TABLE OF CONTENTS

Page

ILLUSTRATIONS

TABLE

CHAPTER 1

INTRODUCTION

If the State Volunteers were the lineal descendants of the county and neighborhood companies that made up the armies of the civil war, the U.S. Volunteers looked forward to the citizen soldier armies of the twentieth century[1]

Brian M. Linn, *The Philippine War: 1899-1902*

In the fall of 1899, General Elwell S. Otis, Commander of US Forces in the Philippines, had been fighting a confusing and costly war for over a year. He had seen tactical successes, but turning tactical success into strategic victory proved very difficult. Some in the United States, most vocally Mark Twain (the noted author) and William Jennings Bryan (President McKinley's political opponent), argued America should give up on its imperial ambitions in the Philippines in favor of concentrating resources on improvements at home.[2]

General Otis believed that a spectacular and visible success against America's former ally, General Emilio Aguinaldo and his Philippine Army of Liberation, would give him the strategic clout he needed to eliminate further Philippine resistance. However, Otis' forces were tired, weakened by disease and had been ineffective in creating support for American rule. Additionally, he had another problem in that the Treaty of Paris was ratified in early 1899. With the agreement that ended the war with Spain and ceded the Philippine Islands to the United States complete, the term of service for the federalized state militia units was also complete. Otis summarized his problem succinctly in June 1899, stating, "Nearly all volunteers [are] inclined to go home; anxious to participate in State welcomes."[3]

1

In the United States, President McKinley was facing an approaching reelection campaign, so he was also looking for good news from abroad, but his military force was stretched too thin to produce the results desired. Consequently, the War Department, along with other military progressives (like Emory Upton and General William T. Sherman) called for an increase in the size of the army. Even the Democrats, most of whom held strong anti-imperialist views, agreed there was a need for more American strength in the Philippines. However, because of the costs associated and the political implications, they did not agree that the strength should come from an increase in the Regular Army.

The thinly stretch Regular Army was already augmented heavily by the "Boys of 98" in Cuba and the Philippines.[4] These units were almost exclusively state militia units that volunteered for temporary federal service. These units signed up to fight for the United States during the surge of patriotism that occurred at the beginning of the Spanish-American War. Unlike the Regulars, these units were raised, organized, officered and trained by their home state governments.

The state regiments experienced a difficult call-up and most units proved to be less prepared than their pre-war bravado suggested. In Philippine combat operations, they performed acceptably. However, the transition from direct combat to counterinsurgency and civil tasks proved daunting. Along with stories of ingenuity, bravery and fierce loyalty in state volunteer units, there were corresponding reports of indiscipline, inconsistency and even criminality. In late 1898, the state volunteers were already growing restless as their enlistments were near completion and they were still far from home.

Congress realized that action had to be taken to bolster the American military ranks, but they could not agree on how to best increase the size of the army. Americans still held a deep-seated distrust of a large army, even if that army was to be employed overseas. Also, the idea of America as an imperial power was a new concept that had not fully taken root in the American psyche. Eventually, after months of political wrangling, Congress arrived at a solution. Congress authorized the President to raise twenty-five new volunteer regiments, under federal control, for a limited term. The deal was political "sausage-making" at its finest. No one side was completely happy, but nearly everyone supported the compromise. By organizing volunteers directly under federal control, the President hoped to avoid the political and practical problems that came along with the use of state militia units.[5] By limiting the terms of the volunteers to two years, the anti-imperialist Congress avoided increasing the size of the standing army. Finally, because this new force would be ready for deployment by October 1899, General Otis could begin plans for new units to replace the worn out "Boys of '98."

In the fall of 1899, thirty-five thousand federal volunteers, the United States Volunteer (U.S.V.) regiments, arrived on the same ships that would take the state militia soldiers home. The military leaders hoped that these twenty-five newly formed regiments (Infantry numbered 26 through 49 and the 11th Cavalry) would give General Otis the operational strength and the fresh legs required to bring decisive strategic victory in the Philippines.[6] Otis' Northern Offensive of the fall of 1899, designed specifically for these new regiments, was to strike deep into the heart of Aguinaldo's strength, his army and his shadow government. If successful, it would allow the United States forces to return to the original task of executing President McKinley's policy of "benevolent assimilation."

Photo Removed Due to Copyright Restrictions

Figure 1.   The Philippines
Source: Wikipedia: *The Free Encyclopedia,* [document on-line]; available from
http://en.wikipedia.org/wiki/Image: Ph_physical_map.png; Internet; accessed on 14
January 2006.

Among the units that arrived in October 1899, the 32nd Infantry Regiment,

United States Volunteers (U.S.V.), has special significance for Fort Leavenworth,

Kansas. This regiment recruited, organized and trained for war in the Eastern Kansas-

Western Missouri area. It established its headquarters at Fort Leavenworth and conducted

its field training in the vicinity of what is now the post driving range. When it departed

for war in September 1899, it participated in a citywide parade through the streets of

Kansas City, MO. Its commander, Colonel Louis A. Craig was a career soldier who hailed from across the Missouri River in Saint Joseph. The 32nd Infantry Regiment's officers were mostly former Kansas and Missouri state militiamen. Filling its ranks were the farmers of the Kansas and Missouri countryside, the sons of bankers and agriculture-businessmen from the city, and everyone in between. During its one and a half years in the Philippines, the 32nd Infantry Regiment found itself involved in several major combat operations. For the most part, however, the 32nd found its niche operating successfully along the northern banks of Manila Bay in the United States Army's first successful counterinsurgency.

Through the history and experiences of the 32nd Infantry Regiment (U.S.V.), this paper examines the U.S. Army Act of 2 March 1899 and the federal volunteer regiments created by this legislation. This thesis will explore key questions related to how this federal volunteer regiment was raised and trained, and it will analyze how it performed in the counterinsurgency mission. Specifically this thesis focus on the following questions: Why did Congress choose federalized volunteers instead of increasing the size or capabilities of the regular force or recruiting more state militia organizations? Based on the history of the 32nd Regiment, once the decision was made to create these organizations how were they recruited, organized, equipped and trained? And finally, based on the history of the 32nd Regiment, did the Army Act of March 1899 create the right kind of organizations to solve the political and military problems of the Philippine Insurrection, 1899 to 1901?

In order to comprehend the rationale behind the Army Act of 1899 and the design of the federal volunteer forces that followed, it is necessary to first understand the context in which the legislation was created. With this in mind, this thesis begins by providing a review of literature to ensure a basic historical understanding of the political, military, economic and cultural climate inside the United States as well as in the Philippines in 1898 and 1899. This review sets the need for this these by showing that the topic has yet to be explored and with worthy of study

This thesis continues in chapter three by providing an overview of the Philippine Insurrection from the strategic and operational level. It discusses General Otis' the need for disciplined troops, the desire for capabilities in civil organization and management, the successes and failures of state militia units. It also provided strategic context to the enemy, General Aguinaldo and his Philippine Army of Liberation (P.A.L.).

The fourth chapter of this paper is designed to discuss the legislative history of the Army Act of 1899 in order to provide the reader with an understanding of the difficult time this legislation faced in Congress. It covers issues such as: the political competition between the War Department, the progressives in the army and the powerful opposition party in Congress, the military culture that existed at the time, and the competition between state and federal governments in relation to military power.

Finally, in order to gain an in-depth and personal perspective, this thesis concludes with the history of one federal volunteer regiment, the 32nd Infantry (U.S.V.). It attempts to follow this regiment from organization in 1899 to demobilization in 1901. The thesis discusses how these soldiers were recruited and how the officers were chosen and it reports on their equipment and organization. The discussion also includes a determination of the training the regiment received prior to their deployment to the Philippines. Once in the Philippine theater, the paper continues its focus on the 32nd

Infantry to determine their capabilities in combat, counterinsurgency and civil-military operations.

Assumptions, Definitions, Limitations, Delimitations and Significance

This paper will closely study the experiences and actions of the 32nd Infantry and it will draw conclusions about the effectiveness of this unit in counterinsurgency. However, the author fully understands that any history, and any conclusion reached, about a specific unit can only be applied cautiously to the entire federal volunteer system or to present day actions. As such, this thesis will draw only broad conclusions to questions related to the entire federal volunteer system.

Two of the most important primary resources for determining the history of the 32nd Infantry are the official reports of Colonel Louis A. Craig and the war diary of Private Karl White. Again, the author understands that each of these writings has inherent biases based on location, position and rank, but this thesis (at least initially) takes these writings to be truthful and accurate.

It is useful to describe, early on, the terms that are used frequently in this thesis. Most important among these are explanations and descriptions of the "Regular Army," the "state militia" and the "National Guard," as they apply to the timeframe of 1898-1901. These terms are described below.

At the time, the Regular Army (also know as "the regulars") was a small professional army that was recruited, trained, officered and resourced by the United States federal government. Although its size varied across the years, the regulars started and ended this period with end strength of around 28,000 soldiers and officers. This army was, however, a peacetime force to be augmented during times of crisis. Before the War with Spain the army spent most of its days guarding western towns and trading outposts and securing the westward expansion of the nation.

The state militia system has it roots in local citizens taking responsibility for local law and order. Essentially, a militia was formed when a group of like-minded citizens recruited their neighbors and formed into a company. Generally, these companies wrote a set of by-laws, elected officers, paid dues, and took to whatever business was at hand.[7] Once organized, the company could apply to their state governor for membership in the state militia. The status of membership in the state organization included state recognition, commissions for their officers and possible financial sponsorship. In return the company was assigned a place in the state military structure and was subject to mobilization by the governor. Under the state militia system, the various state militia units were available for federalization in the case of national invasion or insurrection.[8] At the time, there was a great disparity in how the state governments trained, equipped and employed their militia units. In some cases the militia were not much more than fraternal business-related organizations with little or no military training. In others, they were well-trained, well-drilled and well-equipped. Still others were used more like police-auxiliaries, existing for local law enforcement and riot control situations.

The term National Guard, as it is used in this thesis, applies to an organized collection of professional state militia officers who sought to improve the capabilities and capacity of local military organizations in the late nineteenth century. Seeing the militia system fall apart after the Civil War, the National Guard (and its political lobby, the National Guard Association) worked through federal and state governments to increase funding for state militia, to better organize, equip and train these forces, and to

8

standardize militia units across state boundaries. The purpose of these efforts was to make the organized state militia units an effective citizen-based reserve system to back-up the Regular Army. Although the transformation from individual local units to coherent national organization did not occur overnight, by the time of the Spanish American war, the National Guard had greatly improved the practice of soldiering in the states and garnered itself immense power in both state and federal politics.[9]

The history of the 32nd Infantry is a limited history. Although the law creating federal volunteer regiments was passed in March of 1899, the 32nd, like most U.S.V. units under this mandate, did not begin recruiting until June and did not begin training in earnest until August. Because the 32nd was demobilized in April of 1901, this thesis has a delimited historical scope. The legislative and political history of the Army Act of 1899 obviously includes actions from before this time, as does the context of American and Philippine actions that called for this legislation. However, in general, this paper focuses on the two-year period from early 1899 to early 1901 when the 32nd Infantry (U.S.V.) and the rest of the federal volunteer regiments existed.

In the same manner as current scholarly research focuses on the counterinsurgency to draw tactical and strategic lessons from the Philippine Insurrection, the final chapter of this thesis is designed to draw similar lessons about the organization and character of the forces that engaged in these operations. This thesis will show is that the 32nd was effective in combat, effective in counterinsurgency and exceptionally capable of managing the transitions between the two. In this case, the Army Act of 1899 created an effective organization capable of addressing both the political and the military problems of the Philippine Insurrection.

ENDNOTE ABBREVIATIONS

ANJ   The Army and Navy Journal

CMSR   Compiled Military Service Records (CMSR), 32nd Infantry Regiment
(U.S.V.) Record Group 94, National Archives and Records
Administration, Washington, DC.

KDW   Karl D White, *Diary of Karl D White, Company K, 32nd Infantry
Regiment, United States Volunteers* (Fort Leavenworth, KS: Archives of
the 32nd Infantry Regimental Association).

LES   The Leavenworth Evening Standard

NARA   National Archives and Record Administration. This citation is generally
followed by Record Group Number (RG) and Entry Number from within a
record group (E).

Roster   *Roster of the Thirty-second Infantry: United States Volunteers: Colonel
Louis A. Craig, Commanding, service, 1899, 1900, 1901, Manila,
Philippine Islands.* Regional headquarters, Balanga, Baraan province,
Island of Luzon: 1902. (This book can be found in the rare books
collection, Combined Arms Research Library, Ft Leavenworth, KS.)

RSW   Craig, Louis A., *Report to the Secretary of War from the Thirty-Second
Volunteer Infantry Regiment*, COL Louis A. Craig, Commanding, 1901.
(This narrative is in the personal collection of the Craig family).

---

[1] Brian M. Linn, *The Philippine War: 1899-1902* (Lawrence, Kansas: University Press of Kansas, 2000), 125.

[2] Samuel E. Morrison, et al, *Dissent in Three American Wars (*Cambridge, MA: Harvard University Press, 1970), 78. The Anti-Imperailist League was formed in 1988 to counter what they perceived as adventurous American foreign policy trends. The league was a combination of Democrats and "Mug-Wumps" (fence sitters with their "mug on one side and the wump on the other"). Much more information on the vocal and sometime bitter descent can be found in second chapter of the above-mentioned book.

[3] United States War Department, Adjutant-General's Office. *Correspondence relating to the war with Spain: including the insurrection in the Philippine Islands and the China Relief Expedition, April 15, 1898, to July 30, 1902(Washington D.C.: Government Printing Office, 1905)*, 2:1005.

[4] Dale L. Walker, *The Boys of '98: Theodore Roosevelt and the Rough Riders* (New York: Forge, 1998), 14.

[5] In the first call-up of militia units, problems ranged from dealing with untrained and ill-equipped units to working with politically connected, but tactically ignorant officers. For a greater discussion of these issues see the first chapter of Linn's *The Philippine War.*

[6] Graham A. Cosmas, "Military Reform after the Spanish-American War: The Army Reorganization Fight of 1898-1899." *Military Affairs* 35, No. 1 (February, 1971): 17.

[7] Jerry Cooper, *The Rise of the National Guard (*Lincoln, Nebraska: University of Nebraska Press: 1997), 16.

[8] Linn, 10.

[9] Cooper, 23.

CHAPTER 2

REVIEW OF THE LITERATURE

I speak not of forcible annexation, for that cannot be thought of.
That by our own code of morality would be criminal aggression. [1]

President William McKinley, December 1897

Scores of writers, historians, social scientists and strategists have studied the Philippine Insurrection, the army that fought it, and the disposition of our nation at the time. But, because the topic of this thesis cuts across several different fields of study the review of the literature must do the same. For the purpose of this literature review, works are divided into three distinct categories. These categories are: general military histories of the Spanish-American War and the Philippine Insurrection, research that is specifically focused on the American counterinsurgency operations in the Philippines and discussions of the social and organizational history of the American military at the turn of the twentieth century. This chapter focuses on research that best characterizes the themes listed above. It is by no means comprehensive, nor is it absolute. Instead, the reviews listed in this chapter are the author's choice of works that best represent the scholarship available in each category.

Histories of the Philippine Insurrection

The large shelf of books covering the military and social history of the Spanish-American War and the Philippine Insurrection is daunting. However, Dr. Brian McAllister Linn's influential book *The Philippine War, 1899-1902,* is probably the most effective starting point for any scholar looking to research this field. Dr. Linn is currently

12

a professor of history at Texas A&M University and he holds two prestigious Society for Military History Distinguished Book Awards. Because of this book and its predecessor work, *The U.S. Army and Counterinsurgency in the Philippine* War, 1899-1902, he is often credited with re-invigorating study of the Philippine War. Linn's book, *The U.S. Army and Counterinsurgency*, studied the army's counterinsurgency campaign in Luzon with an impartial eye in an attempt to provide greater context to a conflict that some had labeled America's first Vietnam. In *The Philippine War*, Linn casts a much wider net. It is the comprehensive scope of research that makes *The Philippine War* such an influential history. Linn provides an all-inclusive look at the actions of both the United States army and the Filipino resistance fighters in the first years of the conflict.

Linn opens his book by describing the Battle of Manila and the uncertainty that existed in the mind of the American President. Linn states, "McKinley's uncertainty, his hesitation to commit himself, or the nation, to a policy in the Philippines would place an enormous burden on his military subordinates."[2] This inability to provide a coherent policy would plague American operations for several years.[3] The battle for Manila became an odd three-way operation where the American commanders were ordered to "first overcome the Spanish [in Manila], then shift to block Filipino incursions."[4] Linn argues that ultimate responsibility for the American-Filipino conflict falls on the rebels, but he does not blame Aguinaldo. Instead, the author argues that Aguinaldo was, in many ways, a leader without a constituency and the military situation quickly spiraled out of his control.

Linn makes a concerted effort to describe the dual nature of the mission with which the American military commanders struggled. The Commanding General in the

13

Philippines, Major General Elwell S. Otis, seemed unable to grasp the complexity of the situation. Linn describes Otis as "unable to shift from the narrow focus…of the peacetime army to the demands of war."[5] The difficult tasks required to administer this new nation and fight conventional and guerilla battles fell to the lower level commanders.

If the situation for American forces was difficult, the situation for the Philippine army was worse. Linn describes Aguinaldo as a man who struggled constantly to control his subordinates and the rival factions in his own organization. At the lower levels, repeated defeats against the American forces (particularly defeats where the Americans foolishly, but successfully, charged across open terrain against prepared positions) had deleterious effects on Filipino morale. Given the circumstances, Linn characterizes Aguinaldo's reluctant 1899 decision to resort to a guerilla campaign as sound judgment. In effect, Aguinaldo relinquished what little control he had in favor of additional time and increased initiative at the lower levels of command. However, Linn also concludes that Aguinaldo made a fatal mistake. Because he tied the success of his insurgency to a favorable outcome in the American presidential election in 1900, Aguinaldo used "a strategy suited for a protracted war to achieve an immediate goal."[6] Aguinaldo gained new appeal in the short-term, but incurred widespread demoralization when McKinley was re-elected.

In its final chapters Linn also addresses reports of brutality, torture and a repressive mentality in the American forces, calling them "myths." (This thesis will corroborate Linn's assessment.) He argues against believing them for two reasons. First, he says that "virtually every scholar who has undertaken detailed research in the primary sources" has challenged this mythology. Second, even if brutality did (undoubtedly) occur, it was not endemic to the American forces and challenges the reader to avoid the application of current morality to yesterday's history.[7]

Obviously, no one book can be the final arbiter of events from the past. Just as Dr. Linn's work seems to have replaced its predecessor works as the leading research on the Philippine Insurrection, another book may one day arise to replace this one. Until then, *The Philippine War, 1899-1902* should remain the entry point for any research into this subject.

American Counterinsurgency Actions in the Philippines

In light of ongoing operations in Iraq and Afghanistan, current historical and military scholars have intensified their focus on American actions in the Philippine War in the hopes of drawing lessons from these actions that can be applied to current counter insurgency operations. Although it is a simplistic framework, scholars who are writing about this topic today generally fall into two factions. One side believes that the United States' strategic actions and the actions of its soldiers in the Philippines were unworthy of praise because the cause was not lawful and the tactics employed were brutal. The leading book that follows this line of logic is Stuart C. Miller's *Benevolent Assimilation: The American Conquest of the Philippines*. The other argument acknowledges that some atrocities occurred, but focuses more heavily on the humanitarian reforms and civil-military achievements of our soldiers. The book most often cited by this camp is *Schoolbooks and Krags: The United States Army in the Philippines, 1898-1900*, written by College of Wooster (Wooster, Ohio) Professor, John M. Gates.

Stuart Miller's book, *Benevolent Assimilation*, argues that American actions in the Philippines Insurrection were inept at the highest levels and unabashedly racist and brutal

15

at the lower levels. Strategic ineptitude, Miller argues, caused the American army to

"grossly underestimate the power of national aspirations and the willingness of the enemy

to make unthinkable sacrifices in the face of awesome odds."[8]

However, the most important portion of the book is not what it says about the

leaders, but what it reports about the soldiers. Dr. Miller makes extensive use of personal

letters, diaries and memoirs of soldiers to reveal that patriotism mixed freely with racism

and brutality among soldiers. In addition, the Filipinos had been de-humanized through

racism and the two together led directly to the easy commission of atrocities. One soldier

wrote home that his unit would take "no more prisoners…we will kill [the] wounded and

all of them."[9] Another wrote, "no cruelty is too severe for these brainless monkeys…fill

the blacks with lead before finding out whether they are friends or foe."[10] Miller does not

base all of his conclusions on the writings of soldiers; he also cites official Army reports

that the ratio of dead to wounded Philippine fighters was fifteen-to-one; this is far from

the historical norm which is closer to one dead for every five wounded.[11] Although

official reports from General Otis' office claim superior American marksmanship as the

reason for this discrepancy, Miller's book leaves the reader skeptical of Otis' assertion.

(This thesis supports Otis over Miller, at least on this account.)

Unlike Miller's book, Dr. Gates' research does not emphasize American brutality.

In his opinion, American policy and the soldiers and civil administrators that executed it

were colonial, but generally not barbarous. According to Gates, brutal actions would have

been inconsistent with the need for an organized and compliant population. The

Americans who sought to exploit the Philippines for commercial interests clearly had no intention of doing the manual labor themselves; they wanted an effective worker population with their new colony.

This book makes specific mention of the army's ability to evolve procedures and techniques as the context of the fighting changed. In the beginning, the Army fought the Philippine Army of Liberation (P.A.L.) in conventional battles. As the resistance fighters moved to guerilla operations, the Army focused on isolating the insurgents from the population. To compel acceptance of American rule, Filipinos were offered both positive and negative incentives that were tailored to local situations.[12] American soldiers (like to soldiers of the 32nd) successfully organized municipal governments and created public works such as schools, sewage and health care systems. Essentially, through the emplacement of military units at the village level, conducting daily military and public works activities, the resistance lost traction.

Schoolbooks and Krags points out military conditions in the Philippines prevented extensive management by a higher headquarters in Manila. Great responsibility was placed on commanders down to the company level. Even if benevolence was an official policy, the commanding general could do little to ensure its implementation.[13] However, according to Gates' research, soldiers and leaders at the lowest levels did act with real concern and humane treatment for the Filipino people. Because the lowest level soldiers "acted in a way that fostered pacification even when they were unsupervised or uninformed about the exact nature of official policy," the American pacification efforts were successful.[14]

Social and Organizational History of the Army
at the Turn of the Century

There are numerous scholarly works available to a researcher who attempts to address the nature of military service around the turn of the century. Outstanding among these books are the works of Dr. Edward Coffman, a professor at the University of Wisconsin and Dr. Jerry Cooper, professor at the University of Missouri. Edward Coffman's book, *The Old Army: A Portrait of the American Army in Peacetime, 1784-1898,* provides significant insights into the nature of service for a career soldier during the nineteenth century.[15] Jerry Cooper's book, *The Rise of the National Guard: the Evolution of the American Militia, 1865-1920,* details the evolution of the militia system over 60 turbulent years, as it transformed from local authority to federal control. It also addresses the social and political pressures that created the "citizen-soldier" philosophy that permeates our military policies to this day. Although the scope of these works is far broader than this thesis required, these books are essential reading for any scholar who attempts to draw conclusions about the army of the time.

Less than two decades after the conclusion of the Civil War, the American regular army had shrunk from nearly two million men to under thirty thousand. Coffman explains that an officer who commanded immense Civil War formations at a young age, if he remained in service almost certainly found himself without many soldiers or much of a mission. As the country transitioned from civil war to peace, the army returned to frontier outposts to protect and manage the country's westward expansion. But technologies like railroads and telegraphs made frontier duty a fading task. As the freedoms associated with frontier life diminished, this duty was considered equivalent to punishment (especially as compared to recent wartime experience).[16] Coffman effectively describes

18

the mental and emotional disappointment that came from an officer's deflation of rank, responsibility, and excitement. Coffman further argues that the Civil War and the vanishing frontier were the dominant influences on the army in the last quarter of the nineteenth century.[17]

Soldiers that joined the army in the period before the Spanish-American War generally did so as a "choice of evils." In most cases, civilian life afforded the working class better options, better pay, and higher social status.[18] Because the working classes existed almost exclusively in and around industrialized cities, most army recruitment came from the frontiers and the southern rural states. However, the army retained its presence in the northern cities if for no other reason than to tap the largest pool possible. Economics did play a role in enlistments.

The Old Army spends a great deal of energy discussing the progressive officers of the day. Officers like General Emory Upton and General William Sherman had the vision to see the changing nature of military life and seek professional improvements to their service. Coffman writes, "More than Sherman even, Upton came to symbolize the professional ideal in the regular army."[19] The progressives argued for decades to establish a level of professionalism in the regular army. They believed that new technologies and an ever-expanding nation would call on the military to undertake new missions. If the army failed to professionalize, it would be unable to adapt to changing conditions and doom itself to irrelevance. Although by 1898 the regulars were in no way a fully professional force, the improvements advocated by Upton and instituted by Sherman had notably increased the adaptability, capabilities and effectiveness of the regular army.[20] The creation of federal volunteers in 1899 was a tentative step in the direction of a professional active force.

For its incredible detail and complex storytelling, *The Old Army* is without peer among social histories of the army. It was essential reading for the production of this paper and it remains the premier scholarly work on the army before the Spanish-American War.

In the same manner that *The Old Army* is the best of current research on the regular army, Dr. Jerry Cooper's *The Rise of the National Guard: The Evolution of the American Militia, 1865-1920,* is the best resource available concerning the development of state militia and National Guard units. In this text, Cooper details the organization, operations, evolution and eventual transformation of the American citizen soldier. He uses the term "rise" as a reference to the gradual federalization and professionalization of militia units. Early in his book, Cooper describes local militia units as more fraternal than military. In effect, one could also describe the "rise" of the National Guard as the militarization of uniformed, but distinctly un-military organizations. The essence of *The Rise of the National Guard* is the idea that militia form followed function, and militia functions followed funding. Cooper argues that availability of resources propelled the evolution of the National Guard. As local units could no longer support themselves, they looked to their states for financial sponsorship. In return the state governments stipulated the type of units required and the missions such units would undertake. As the states expanded the requirements placed on their militia, resources again became scarce and militia units bound together to seek federal sponsorship as a National Guard. Again funding incurred new obligations and oversight. Thus, over the sixty years that followed

20

the civil war, our national militia structure evolved from self-supporting, independent, localized volunteer forces to a centralized state/national military force largely funded by the federal government.[21] The federal volunteers straddled the militia and regular systems.

It was in these times that the idea of a National Guard was born. States began to realize that maintaining a standing militia for infrequent work was expensive and inefficient. In the 1880s, several state leaders sought federal assistance to maintain their forces as a reserve for the regular army. Because the regulars thought of the militia as more business associations than they were military organizations, they overlooked state militia units and argued for a military policy that raised new, federal volunteers in times of crisis. However, many state militia leaders, being from the well-connected business and aristocrat classes of society, wielded more influence over Congressional opinions than did the regulars. Over the next two decades, the militia lobby persuaded Congress to accept the premise of an organized national reserve and begin fiscal sponsorship of some state militia. The Regular Army, in turn, was directed to provide professional sponsorship in terms of training and equipment. Thus began the true National Guard.[22]

Like *The Old Army, The Rise of the National Guard* is an indispensable work for any scholar looking to study the intricacies of the military before 1900. The militia system and the citizen soldier have been the mainstay of our nation's military structure for a most of our history and these state-militias contributed the majority of the soldiers who fought the early days of the Philippine War. Without an understanding of these units it would be impossible to draw conclusions about the U.S. Volunteers that replaced them in the villages and countrysides of Luzon.

Conclusions

The purpose of this chapter was to describe the key scholarly works that are relevant to study of United States federal volunteers in the Philippine Insurrection. Oddities among military units, these regiments were neither state militia nor regular army. They were federal units filled with volunteer soldiers. The federal volunteer regiments were fleeting organizations. They had no history and no future. Not only did they lack unit legacies to inspire their soldiers; they were disbanded within two years of their creation. Yet, in 1899 and 1900, the United States Volunteer Infantry Regiments bore the preponderance of the American national effort in the Philippines. Because of their nature, an effective literature survey concerning these regiments cuts across several disciplines of study. In such a survey it is rare to draw a clear conclusion from the review. However, what can be noted is that minimal research has been directed specifically on these organizations. Also, this review shows that no research can be complete without reviews of many different social and organizations facets of the country and the military in the late nineteenth century.

---

[1] William McKinley, *Annual Message of the President to Congress,* December 6 1897, The American Presidency Project, University of California, Santa Barbara, http://www.presidency.ucsb.edu/ws/index.php?pid=29538 (accessed 11 Jan 2006). In this case, President McKinley is speaking specifically of the annexation of Cuba, but these words would be used against him less that a year later in debates about the annexation of the Philippines.

[2] Linn, *The Philippine War*, 5.

[3] As an example of the disjointedness of the policy, Linn describes the irony that the same American forces that returned Aguinaldo from exile in Hong Kong wound up fighting him during their attempt to consolidate naval successes into control on the land.

[4] Linn, *The Philippine War*, 25.

[5] Ibid., 101.

[6] Ibid., 186.

[7] Ibid., 322.

[8] Stuart Creighton Miller, *Benevolent Assimilation: The American Conquest of the Philippines, 1899-1903,* (New Haven, CT: Yale University Press, 1982 .268. The book describes the Commanding General in the Philippines, General Otis, as cautious, deskbound and universally disrespected by his subordinates.

[9] Ibid., 188.

[10] Ibid., 189.

[11] Ibid.

[12] John Morgan Gates, Schoolbooks *and Krags: The United States Army in the Philippines, 1898-1902,* (Westport, CT: Greenwood Press, 1973) 270.

[13] Ibid., 284.

[14] Ibid., 284.

[15] Coffman's companion piece, *The Regulars: The American Army, 1898-1941,* captures a similar history for the army in the first half of the twentieth century.

[16] Edward M. Coffman, *The Old Army: A Portrait of the American Army in Peacetime, 1784-1898,* (New York: Oxford University Press, 1986), vii 217.

[17] Ibid., 218.

[18] Ibid., 329.

[19] Ibid., 272.

[20] Ibid., 273.

[21] Cooper, *The Rise of the National Guard,* xiii.

[22] Ibid., 42.

CHAPTER 3

THE PHILIPPINE INSURRECTION

It should be the earnest and paramount aim of the military
administration to win the confidence, respect, and affection of the
inhabitants of the Philippines…and by proving to them that the
mission of the United States is one of benevolent assimilation,
substituting the mild sway of justice and right for arbitrary rule.[1]

President William McKinley, 21 December 1898

The purpose of this thesis is not to describe the American policies and Filipino

actions that led to the Philippine Insurrection. Nor is the purpose to detail the successes or

failures on either side of the dispute. The focus of this thesis falls squarely on one of the

federal volunteer regiments that took part in successful counterinsurgency operations in

the Philippines from 1899-1901. However, within that focus, we cannot fully

comprehend the political and military situation the members of the 32nd Infantry U.S.V.

experienced without knowledge of the greater operation around them. The following

chapter provides a cursory review of event leading to the Philippine insurrection and the

military and civil actions that occurred during the height of this conflict. It is not intended

to be complete--far longer and more detailed works already exist on the larger subject.

This chapter serves as a description of what this author believes to be the salient events of

the Philippine insurrection.

Start of the Conflict

Unrest in the Philippines did not begin with the introduction of American forces

in the region; instead it began with the previous occupying power, the Spanish. In the mid

1800's, after nearly 300 years under colonial rule, many European-educated Filipinos began attempting to rectify the great inequalities that existed between the Spanish people and the people of their colony. Because Spanish rule was the system under which they were educated, these educated Filipinos--known as *Illustrados*--sought local reforms, not independence. Their primary goal was representation as a state within the Spanish government, as most believed statehood would give the Filipinos adequate voice and control over their own destiny.

Growing out of the Illustrado movement, a secret society, the *Kapitunan,* gained prominence in the Filipino reform movement. The Kapitunan espoused complete independence from the Spanish crown and, as such ideas were illegal, its members remained underground. As the Kapitunan grew in size and capability, a young and charismatic leader named Emilio Aguinaldo rose to power from within it ranks. General Aguinaldo pushed the movement out of the shadows, beyond rhetoric into action. Thus began the Filipino revolt against Spanish rule. In September and November 1896, Aguinaldo and his small army defeated the Spanish regulars on the battlefield, but the Spanish learned quickly. For another year, the Filipino insurgents fought bloody battles against the better organized and equipped Spanish troops. They pushed the insurgent fighters into the hills and sued for peace. The December 1897 Pact of Biacnabato ended to the revolt, reestablished Spanish control over the Philippines, disassembled the insurgent army and exiled the young General Aguinaldo to Hong Kong. [2]

Around the same time, in the western hemisphere, relations between the Spanish and the Americans were declining and the McKinley Administration was eager to flex American muscle in local waters (the Caribbean Sea). On 15 February 1898 in Havana Bay, an explosion on Battleship Maine and its subsequent sinking provided the impetus for war with the Spain.[3] The major battles in this war would take place in the Spanish western colonies of Puerto Rico and Cuba.

Americans versus Spanish versus Filipinos

As tensions mounted between the Spanish and the Americans in mid April 1898, the U.S. Counselor General in Singapore, Spencer Pratt, met with Aguinaldo in exile and offered a verbal promise of Philippine independence. In return, Aguinaldo would be transported to the Philippines Islands and incite the people against the Spanish.[4] On 30 April 1898, just four days after the United States declared war on Spain, Admiral George Dewey and the American naval fleet in Asia destroyed the dilapidated Spanish-Philippine fleet in its homeport at Manila Bay. Dewey also destroyed Spanish gun coastal artillery emplacements, but without significant infantry forces he could do little to control the city of Manila.

While the American army steamed to the Philippines from California, Dewey blockaded the port of Manila and arranged for General Aguinaldo's return to his homeland. Dewey's forces delivered Aguinaldo and his lieutenants to Cavite (a city in Northern Luzon) on May 19 and immediately the Philippine independence movement became energized once again. Aguinaldo quickly rebuilt his "Army of Liberation" and gathered his troops around Spanish-controlled Manila. While Dewey waited for reinforcements to arrive, Aguinaldo established military control over the Luzon countryside.[5] Although the Filipinos and Americans shared a common goal in the defeat of Spanish forces, their relationship soured through the summer months. Aguinaldo expected liberty for the Philippine people (under his control, of course), and as such had already created a provincial government and declared Filipino independence. President

McKinley, however, was beginning to believe that the islands should remain under American control.[6] In August, when the American forces under Major General Wesley Merritt arrived and captured Manila, the city was immediately declared off-limits to the Filipino insurgent army while the McKinley administration was determining its Philippine policy. Aguinaldo was informed that Pratt did not have the authority to offer independence and, accordingly, the American government recognized only Aguinaldo's military leadership, not his civil authority.[7]

Figure 2.   Emilio Aguinaldo
Source: National Archives (Photo No. 111-SC-98358)

After the Spanish were defeated in the Caribbean, in the south Pacific (Hawaii and Guam) and in the Philippines, the United States and Spanish governments began negotiations for peace. While the peace negotiations continued, the United States policy in the Philippines remained undecided. The United States and the Philippine Army of Liberation fell into an uneasy truce--Merritt in control of Manila and Manila Bay and

27

Aguinaldo in control of nearly everything else. In December, when the Treaty of Paris was signed and the war between United States and Spain officially concluded, it became apparent to Aguinaldo that the United States intended to annex the Philippines. In his now famous "Benevolent Assimilation" speech (part of which is quoted at the beginning of this chapter), President McKinley ordered the subjugation of the Philippine Islands under the new American empire.

Conventional War against Aguinaldo

On February 4, 1899, an American force consisting mostly of state militia units opened fire on an insurgent patrol that had crossed into disputed territory and the American-Filipino relationship erupted into war. The new American commander, Major General Elwel Otis (formerly, Merritt's second-in-command), seized upon this opportunity to attack the Filipino trenches and take high ground surrounding his current lines.[8] News of the skirmishes reached the United States as Congress was debating both the Treaty of Paris and plans to increase the size of the Army.[9]

Through the spring of 1899, General Otis focused his military operations in Northern Luzon, where he felt the Filipinos were the strongest.[10] He steadily pushed the insurgent army away from major cities and into the hills. However, with every success on the battlefield, Otis' Eighth Corps moved further from Manila. As the army extended its position, it required more soldiers to guard supply lines and protect communications. By mid April, the Eighth Corps had only 16,000 soldiers available for duty on the island of Luzon, a number far too small to control the both Manila and the Philippine interior simultaneously.[11]

Aguinaldo was an educated man and a student of the European armies of the day. As such, his P.A.L. showed great competence in building fortifications, trench-works and defensive positions. However, his army lacked the training methods that led to discipline and increased marksmanship. The American soldiers quickly learned that open order tactics and quick maneuver would break a Filipino resistance line nearly every time. Aguinaldo also ascribed to a strategy that ceded territory before taking heavy casualties. He understood that the American army did not have the strength to hold terrain and every American incursion into the countryside would inevitably be followed by a withdrawal to supply lines. At a convenient time the insurgents would simply filter back and regain what was territory lost.

The status of Otis' soldiers further complicated his problems. Fully half of his forces were state militia units whose military obligation officially ended in April. The War Department had already instructed Otis the militia should be "sent home at the moment you feel they can be spared." But, with ranks thin and the insurgent army active, the soldiers could not be spared.[12] The arrival of several of Regular regiments in May did little to mollify Otis' problems. These regulars were not the experienced soldiers that fought with General Merritt's forces a year earlier. Instead, most of these soldiers had enlisted only months earlier.[13] General Otis was forced to consolidate his troops around Manila and wait for help. That help was scheduled to arrive in the fall in the form of twenty-five new federal volunteer regiments.

In the October 1899, thirty-five thousand federal volunteers, the United States Volunteer (U.S.V.) regiments, arrived on the same ships that would take the state militia soldiers back home. The military leaders hoped that these twenty-five newly formed regiments (Infantry numbered 26 through 49 and the 11th Cavalry) would give General Otis the operational strength and the fresh legs required to bring decisive strategic victory in the Philippines.[14] Otis' Northern Offensive of the fall of 1899, designed specifically for these new regiments, was to strike deep into the heart of Aguinaldo's strength, his army and his shadow government. If successful, it would allow the United States forces to return to the original task of executing President McKinley's policy of "benevolent assimilation."

Otis devised a three-pronged plan in which one column (commanded by Major General Arthur MacArthur and including the 32nd Regiment, U.S.V.) would push north from Manila in order to fix the insurgent army on the Pampanga Plain. A second column (under Major General Henry W. Lawton) would march east and then north to meet the third column (under Medal of Honor winner, Major General Loyd Wheaton) that was to be transported by boat to the shores of the Lingayen Gulf.

The tactical intent of this operation was to seal the insurgent army from escape to the mountains of northern Luzon and destroy them in the field.[15] Although Otis' Northern offensive was not successful in capturing the leadership of the P.A.L., it was able to destroy the majority of its conventional field forces. As a result, Aguinaldo was never again able to mount a conventional campaign against the United States forces.Despite this defeat, Aguinaldo remained optimistic.

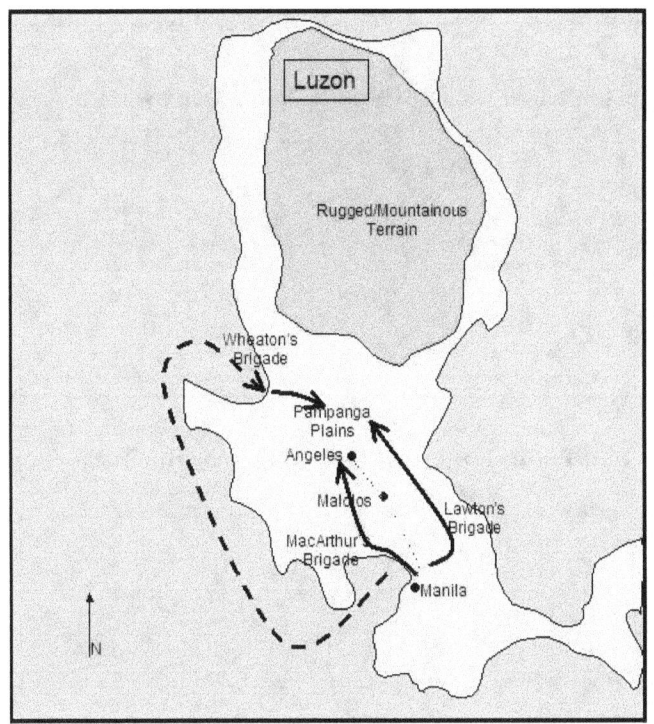

Figure 3.   Otis' Northern Offensive, November 1899

He was an astute student of American politics and recognized that the anti-imperialist sentiment in the United States was growing and President McKinley was under serious political competition from his presidential rival, William Jennings Bryan. Aguinaldo believed that he could still win by keeping the Filipino population committed to his cause and by keeping the American forces sufficiently occupied for one more year. After that year, the American voters would surely remove McKinley and Bryan would grant the Philippines its independence. In most areas, the Filipino insurgents suspended aggressive combat operations in favor of operations that helped them better control the population. While the American forces based themselves near their magazines and conducted "hikes" into the hills and jungles, the insurgents moved into the towns and

31

created shadow governments. The insurgents collected taxes, established organized resistance and even established their own punitive justice system.[16]

Photo Removed Due to Copyright Restrictions

Figure 4.   A Patrol Advances During Otis' Northern Offensive, November 1899
Source: William Dinwiddie, Harper's Weekly, Dec. 23, 1899.

Counterinsurgency

When Otis was relieved and MacArthur took command in the spring of 1900, life for the soldiers began to change. MacArthur pushed his army into the countryside, where it stayed. He established a system of districts, each controlled by a regiment, where coordinated military and civic actions could take place. The American forces set camps in the towns and villages and began to interact with the population. The Americans brought expertise, money and labor to build schools, roads and communication networks. They also aggressively pursued insurgents whenever they showed themselves. The eventual victory of the American army can be attributed not only to the intensity of their military operations, but also to the American soldier's ability to embed and interact with the population, thereby dislodging the influence of the insurgents and their shadow governments. The American soldier was trained for combat but spent much of his time building schools, training police and establishing local governance. During the 1902 Senate hearings into the affairs in the Philippines (unofficially called the "Lodge Commission"), William Howard Taft, the President's appointed Governor of the Philippine Commission) commented on the difficult task.

> Now when you consider the difficulties…in furnishing, in a country infested with guerilla bands in a country practically without roads, the quartermaster supplies and commissary supplies for 500 different outposts, the escorts that were necessary, and combine with that the duty of chasing the guerilla bands from point to point in impassable mountains, you can see what a tremendous task the army had. And as you look back it is most remarkable that it succeeded as it did; and insurgents were chased with an activity and a skill and an ability that was of great surprise to them…The insurgents were finally, by the energy of the troops, made very tired of guerilla warfare.[17]

By the middle of 1900, when the Philippine counterinsurgency started to achieve success, the great majority of the American soldiers were from the Volunteer Army. The federal volunteer regiments, like the 32nd Infantry U.S.V., were a grand experiment and their progress was closely monitored. Major General Henry Corbin, the Adjutant General, seemed to believe in their eventual success when in his 1899 annual report he noted, "The reports and inspection of these regiments since organization show them to be efficient and possessed of excellent material, both in officers and enlisted men; in truth it is not too much to say that better volunteer regiments have never been organized."[18] In a report to Secretary of War, Elihu Root, in 1900, Governor-General Taft further described operations is the Philippines, stating, "the pacification of the islands seems to depend largely on the character of the military officer in charge of the particular district."[19] In general, these federally recruited, trained and led volunteers proved to have the right mix

of leadership, experience and talent to be successful in this counterinsurgency.

---

[1] William McKinley, *Benevolent Assimilation Proclamation,* December 21 1898, The Philippine Centennial Celebration Website, Laguna, P.I., http://www.msc.edu.ph/centennial/benevolent.html (accessed 16 Jan 2006).

[2] Brian M. Linn*, The U.S. Army and Counterinsurgency in the Philippine War, 1899-1902*, (Chapel, Hill, NC: The University of North Carolina Press, 1989), 4-7.

[3] It was later learned that the explosion was caused by an internal fire and the Spanish had nothing to do with the sinking.

[4] A. B. Feuer, *America at War: The Philippines, 1898-1913,* (Westport, CT: Praeger Publishers, 2002), page *xx.*

[5] Richard W. Stewart, ed. *American Military History Volume I: The United States Army and the Forging of a Nation, 1775-1917* Center of Military History, Washington D.C., 352.

[6] Feuer, page *xx.*

[7] Ibid.

[8] Ibid., 354.

[9] As this news arrived in the United States--recalling that these were the days of "yellow journalism"--it, no doubt, helped secure treaty ratification and increased pressure on Congress to pass an army size increase.

[10] Linn, *The Philippine War*, 88.

[11] Ibid., 89.

[12] Ibid.

[13] Ibid., 90. Among the 9th and 20th Regular Infantry Regiments, less than one in five soldiers had previous combat experience.

[14] Cosmas, "Military Reform After the Spanish-American War", 17.

[15] Stewart, 356.

[16] Linn, *The U.S. Army and Counterinsurgency*, 40.

[17] William H. Taft, *Hearings before the Committee on the Philippines of the United States Senate*, February 4, 1902.

[18] United States War Department, *Annual Reports of the War Dept. 1899*, (Washington D.C.: Government Printing Office, 1900) I:2, 21.

[19] Linn, *The U.S. Army and Counterinsurgency*, 22.

CHAPTER 4

THE LEGISLATIVE HISTORY OF THE ARMY ACT OF 1899

> It is my purpose to muster out the entire Volunteer Army as soon as the Congress shall provide for the increase of the regular establishment. This will be only an act of justice and will be much appreciated by the brave men who left their homes and employments to help the country in its emergency.[1]

> President William McKinley, December 1898

By 1898, when the armistice to end hostilities with Spain was signed, the size of the active federal force had ballooned to nearly 200,000 troops. Most of these soldiers, however, were state militiamen on a limited stint of federal duty specifically designed to fight the war with Spain. Their service would end with the ratification of a peace treaty with Spain. Recognizing the impending decline, political and military leaders from nearly all viewpoints understood that they needed to improve the size and capability of the army if they planed to effectively police the newly acquired American lands. The army's regular strength of 28,000 was not enough to meet its new responsibilities.[2] Without maintaining a large number of the state militiamen or drastically increasing the regular army size, the United States could be in peril of losing its newly inherited empire to chaos. How to best accomplish this expansion was the order of the day and the Army Act of 1899, creating twenty-five federalized volunteer regiments, became an important early step in the eventual complete overhaul of the American "army for empire."[3]

Calls for Expansion and Reform

Even before the Spanish-American War there were calls for reform and growth inside the army. Civil War hero, General William Sherman, had been calling for increased professionalization of the army as early as the 1870s.[4] General Emory Upton (whose ideas were the model by which future Secretary of War Elihu Root would eventually reorganize the army) called for the army to have the ability to rapidly expand during wartime. He also advocated the creation of professional school, journals, and associations. Under Upton's model, officers would be promoted based on merit instead of political connections and a strategic planning staff would be established at the army headquarters to manage the ever-expanding demand for trained land forces.[5]

President McKinley's administration based their original army expansion plans on the reformist proposals coming from these progressive thinkers. They sought to raise a sizeable force under federal control not only to address concerns wartime concerns, but also to begin an army reform process. The McKinley War Department also sought to avoid an over-reliance on state militias who most in the regular force considered of doubtful reliability. In early 1898, at the beginning of the War with Spain, the War Department proposed a force of 104,000 regular troops. This force, they believed, would be substantial enough to defeat the Spanish armies in Puerto Rico, Cuba, and the Philippines.[6]

The National Guard Association (the political lobby of most state militiamen) was stronger in congress than the War Department had anticipated. They opposed this proposal strongly, calling for the use and federal funding of the standing state militia units to address the national threats.[7] In another setback for the War Department, a frugal congress resisted nearly all efforts to expand the regular army. In April 1898, at the end of the legislative cycle, congress passed an initial bill designed to create an army to fight Spain. This law created a volunteer force that would be organized by the states and led by officers appointed by state governors--they would be paid for and deployed by the federal government. Under this plan, the standing state militia units were expected to volunteer *en masse* to serve the country. Theses units would be federally funded, but would retain their state affiliation.

By the end of 1898, the volunteer force of state militia units (also known as the "Boys of 98") totaled nearly 125,000 men and the regular force reached nearly 65,000.[8] Under a deal that placated the cost-sensitive congress, all but the original 28,000 regular troops would be discharged from federal service upon a proclamation of peace with Spain.

Because nearly everyone would be discharged with two years, the new army structures did little to alleviate War Department concerns over how to police the new empire. Less than 6 months after the difficult congressional fight for volunteers, Secretary of War Russell Alger re-opened the discussion. In his 1898 annual address, Secretary Alger called for the regular army to be permanently increased to 100,000 officers and men. As his principle reason for the increase, he cited the "needs of a military force in the islands occupied by the United States."[9] The uniformed officers at the head of the army echoed their Secretary's call in their public statements and reports. When President McKinley offered his "unqualified approval" for the army strength increase, the weight of the office of the President raised the discussion to new levels and started the legislative campaign.[10]

Other noteworthy military officers added their support to the cause. General John Schofield, a two-time war hero (Mexican and Civil wars), added his considerable prestige to the issue. Even the U.S. Navy's greatest theorist, Captain Alfred Thayer Mahan, stressed the need for "and adequate and extremely mobile army." [11] The National Guard, whose leadership was satisfied with the previous year's state militia in call-ups, was also no longer opposed to the enlargement of the regular army. [12]

Staff reform was also high on the list of changes to be made to an expanded army. Included in the potential reforms were adaptations to the policy that assigned officers permanently to the army's administrative sections, or "bureaus". [13] Because the bureaus reported directly to the Secretary of War, the Commanding General of the Army had no authority over the actions of these staffs even though their actions directly impacted those units on the front lines. Most officers (outside the bureaus) believed that permanent assignment to bureaus led to policies uninformed by the realities of the regular army. Another problem that reformers sought to address was the lack of a true commander of the army. Under the structure designed in the Civil War, the Commanding General of the Army controlled all troops of the line, but had no planning staff of his own and no authority over supply, administration and other functions. [14] Further, the relationship between the Commanding General and the Secretary of War depended solely on personalities. There was no basis in law that dictated who worked for whom, under the President. Disagreements between the Commanding General, Major General Nelson A. Miles, and Secretary Alger occured publicly and often. This led Alger to rely on the Adjutant-General, Brigadier General Henry Corbin, as his de facto link to the army.

Although it was Corbin and Alger (with the support of Representative John Hull) who drafted and proposed the primary legislation for army reform in 1898, the atmosphere was charged with reform ideas. Three major bills would be proposed in late 1898 and many representatives and senators proposed their own alternative variations or amendments to those three bills.

Competing Army Reform Bills

On 5 December 1898, Major General Miles, who had been circumvented in the authorship of the Hull bill, presented his version of army reform to Secretary Alger. Miles' plan also called for a regular force of about 100,000 troops. These soldiers, however, were to be organized into an increased number of smaller regiments. The increased number of regiments would require a corresponding increase in officer promotions and an increase in the span of control of the Commanding General and his staff. Consequent to this new span of control, Miles believed that the Commanding General should be awarded the four-star rank of a full general. Although the Miles bill avoided a complete overhaul of the army staff and bureau system, it did take a step towards improving the efficiency of that system by filling vacancies in the Adjutant-General's office and the Quartermaster's office with officers on rotation from the line.[15] Secretary Alger forwarded Miles' version to both houses of Congress--without his endorsement. Without the active support of the Secretary of War or any major representatives or senators, the Miles Bill stood little chance of passage.

Two days later, Congressman Hull introduced the (Corbin-Alger designed) army reform bill in the House of Representatives. The bill provided for an enlisted strength of about 100,000 regular soldiers the majority of whom would be assigned to infantry, cavalry, and artillery regiments. As for staff reorganization, it promoted the Commanding General of the Army from Major General to Lieutenant General and it assigned more officers to the administrative bureaus. Probably because a bureau chief (Corbin) was a primary author, the Hull bill ignored issues related to unity of command or army headquarters staff reorganization.[16]

The next week, a third plan entered the political fray when Representative George McClellan Jr. introduced his version of an army reform bill.[17] The McClellan bill, like the previous two and the prevailing national sentiment, called for a regular force of around 100,000 men. In opposition to the competing bills, Representative McClellan took direct aim at the headquarters of the army and the War Department. Most notably, his plan consolidated the bureaus of the Inspector-General and the Adjutant-General to create a high-level staff with overall responsibility to plan, organize and coordinate army operations.[18] Officers who served on this staff would hold permanent appointments, but these appointments could only be granted after five years of successful line service. Those appointed to staff duty would also be required to return to troop duty for two of every ten years. Finally, the McClellan plan subordinated the supply bureaus to the Lieutenant General commanding the army. The Commanding General of the Army, in turn, was to be subordinate to the Secretary of War.

While the desire for an increase of army strength corresponded with the increase overseas requirements, it also was consistent with the army's newfound prestige. The American public afforded the uniformed army, more than any other organization, credit for victory in the Spanish American War and for consolidating the new empire of the United States. On the other hand, the War Department, specifically the civilian leadership of the War Department, was perceived to be in shambles.[19] Included in the administrative and organizational disasters were massive epidemics among the troops overseas, shortages of training equipment and charges of corruption that reached the highest levels.[20] This dichotomy played out in the rift between the Commanding General Miles (who represented the uniformed army) and the Secretary of War Alger (who represented the civilian leadership of the War Department). The public and the political leaders overwhelmingly sided with the General. This rift and the confusion over reform of the army would play a significant role in the legislative negotiations that were to follow.

Table 1. Comparison of Key Army Bills, 1898-1899			
	Senator Hull's Bill	General Miles' Bill	Representative McClellan's Bill
Regular Army Strength	100,000	100,000	100,000
Regiments	Fill existing regiments to capacity	More regiments of decreased size	Fill existing regiments to capacity
Commanding General Rank	Lieutenant General	Full General	Lieutenant General
Commanding General subordinate to Secretary of War?	No	No	Yes
Bureau System	No changes	Bureau officers rotated from the line	Consolidate bureaus into an "Army Staff"; Bureau officers required return regularly to the line

Actions in Congress

Although both sides of the aisle favored expansion of the army, all the bills "ran afoul of a complex of political forces."[21] Military reformers were quick to point out the lack of true organizational change in most plans. The press and the public were leery of anything that came out of a War Department they perceived to be inept. And the Democratic Party in Congress was quick to conflate the permanent increases and reorganization in the standing army to a greater issue – the annexation of the Philippines.[22]

In December 1898, while others in Congress pushed whichever bill they supported, no bill had near the political support that the Hull bill enjoyed. As the Chairman of the House Committee on Military Affairs, Representative Hull exercised his bureaucratic powers to restrict the deliberations of his committee to his own legislation. The committee heard testimony from military and civilian leaders, nearly all of which agreed with permanent end-strength increases. There were, however, significant disagreements about staff and command reform. On a party-line vote, the committee's Republican majority sent the bill to the floor with a recommendation for approval.[23]

The Democrats on the Military Affairs Committee quickly drafted a dissenting report that focused on the imperialist implications of permanently increasing the size of the standing army. Of the 100,000-man regular force, the dissenting reported stated, "Such an army is not necessary to be maintained in this country now, neither because of our relations to the islands of the sea nor because of any necessity which…has arisen in this country itself."[24] In essence, most Democrats argued that the future of the Philippines, Cuba and Puerto Rico had not been determined and therefore it would be reckless to raise a significantly sized permanent army. The dissenting report, along with a minority proposal to grant the President an authority to temporarily increase the army by 50,000 volunteers, served notice to the majority that the minority was willing to fight over military reform.

Because Representative Hull had fallen temporarily ill, the House of Representatives did not debate the competing bills on the floor until late January when, at the same time, the Senate was debating ratification of the Treaty of Paris. As could be expected, Republicans supported the Hull Bill in a bloc and most Democrats rejected it. This gave the bill a majority of support in the House. The Democrats, however, were not without success in the debates. They were able to gain consensus that the Philippines needed defending, but that the islands were most threatened by external attacks that would undoubtedly come from the sea. Following this logic, they agued that any increase in ground forces was a backdoor designed to create an imperialist force to subjugate the Philippine people.[25] Although the House eventually did pass the Hull Bill in an amended form, the Democrats were able to tie the issue of army reform inextricably to American imperialism in the Philippines.

The Senate, having completed most of its Treaty of Paris debate, took up the issue of army reform. On 4 February, two days before officially ratifying of the Treaty of Paris, the Senate debated the Hull Bill. On the same day across the globe, a skirmish between U.S. and Philippine troops outside of Manila ignited into war. Under this new pressure, Senator Joseph Hawley, the Republican Chairman of the Senate Committee on Military Affairs, pushed his committee to approve the Hull bill quickly. Unfortunately for the

Republicans, one of their members was out of the country and the committee deadlocked in a five-to-five vote.

In mid-February 1899, the Senate Committee on Military Affairs sent two distinct plans to the floor for consideration, the Hull bill and a Democratic alternative. The Democratic substitute allowed the President to maintain the current regular force of 65,000 men until July 1901. It also authorized the President to raise an additional force of 35,000 soldiers composed of native volunteers serving in their homelands of Puerto Rico, Cuba or the Philippines.[26]

With the Congressional session nearing a close, the Democrats made it clear that they intended to block the Hull bill in favor of their temporary solution. The War Department, bolstered by press reports that President McKinley was planning to stake his political clout on the Hull bill passage, issued a statement that dismissed the Democratic alternative. Secretary Alger argued that the plan to use native troops was unrealistic because those soldiers would likely prove unreliable.[27] With ten days left in the Congressional session and nine appropriation bills yet to pass, the Republicans in the Senate backed down and began a bargaining process.

Final Resolution

On the night of the 23 February, Republican Senator Joseph Hawley, Democratic Senator Francis Cockrell and a representative of the army's Adjutant-General's office hammered out a compromise bill palatable to all parties. The final plan called for the regular army to continue at its current size of 65,000 troops until July 1901. It provided the President with authority to expand the active army to face current challenges by raising 25 new volunteer regiments under federal control. The addition of these regiments amounted to an increase of 35,000 soldiers in service until July 1901.[28] Most importantly, these additional volunteer soldiers would not come from the state forces. Instead, they were to be directly recruited, organized, trained and officered under federal control. These units were the first truly national volunteers of the new American empire.

The Democratic minority was pleased with this new law because it proved that they were able to foil majority plans when the need arose. The Republican majority was pragmatic and believed this bill was they best they could do considering the circumstances. Only the military reformers were unhappy. Although the bill included steps to improve army tactical structures, command and staff issues remained undressed. Congressman Hull called the Army Act of 1899 "the worst kind of patchwork," and even Rough-Rider, Theodore Roosevelt called the new legislation a "miserable makeshift."[29]

On the 27 February the Senate passed the Army bill and on the 2 March 1899, President McKinley signed the Army Act of 1899, setting into motion a grand experiment in manning of an army of a democratic society. According to Dr. Linn in his seminal book, *The Philippine War*, "if state volunteers were the lineal descendants of the neighborhood companies that made up the Civil War armies, then the U.S. Volunteers looked forward to the national citizen soldier armies of the twentieth century."[30] In looking back, it is easy to see this connection. But the participants at the time could not have imagined the precedent they set by creating and employing federal volunteer military organizations. To Hull, McClellan, Alger and Miles, the nation was at risk of losing its hard fought gains and they were simply solving an immediate problem.

[1] William McKinley, *Annual Message of the President to Congress*, Dec 5 1898, The American Presidency Project, University of California, Santa Barbara http://www.presidency.ucsb.edu/ws/print.php?pid=29539, (accessed 11 Jan 2006).

[2] Edward Coffman, *The Regulars: The American Army, 1898-1941(Cambridge, MA: Harvard University Press, 2004), chapter 1.*

3 Graham A. Cosmas, *An Army For Empire: The United States Army in the Spanish American War* (Columbia, MO: University of Missouri Press, 1994), 3.

[4] Coffman, *The Old Army*, 272.

[5] Upton, Emory, *The Military Policy of the United States* (Senate Document #494, 62nd congress, 2nd session, Washington D.C.: Government Printing Office, 1904).

[6] Cosmas, *Military Reform*, 13.

[7] Cooper, *The Rise of the National Guard*, Chapter 4.

[8] Cosmas, *Military Reform*, 13.

[9] United States War Department, *Annual Reports of the War Dept. 1898.*

[10] Cosmas, *Military Reform*, 13.

[11] Mahan, Alfred T. *Lessons of the War with Spain and Other Articles* (Boston: Little, Brown, 1899), 16-17.

[12] Cosmas, *Military Reform*, 13. It is worth noting that many of the predictions of the inadequacy and low readiness in the state militias were found to be true, so many of the National Guard leaders were preoccupied with their own reforms.

[13] The bureaus were the staff organizations that ran the administrative, logistical, engineering, investigative, and judicial functions of the army.

[14] Ibid.

[15] Ibid.

[16] Ibid., 14.

[17] George B. McClellan, *McClellan's Own Story: the War for the Union*, (Charles Webster and Company, New York., 1886), 650. George McClellan Jr. was the son of a Civil War general and after his Congressional service McClellan Jr. was elected the Mayor of New York City. His family name held great prestige in New York area. Undoubtedly, Representative McClellan's perceptions of the army and the command

structure the War Department were shaped by study of his father's experiences. His father, General George McClellan, was an outstanding organizer and trainer but was widely considered to be overly cautious in war. According to his memoirs, General McClellan felt as if he never truly gained the trust of President Lincoln or the full support of the War Department. In 1862 (after failing to pursue General Lee at the Battle of Antietam) McClellan was publicly dismissed from the position of Commander-in-Chief of the Union Armies. In civilian political life, General McClellan (a Democrat) would challenge, but fail to defeat, Lincoln in the 1864 presidential election. He also would serve as the governor of New Jersey

[18] Cosmas, *Military Reform,* 14.

[19] The New York Times, 9 Dec 1898, 1.

[20] For more on the problems associated with the call up of state militias see U.S. Congress. Senate. *Report of the Commission Appointed by the President to Investigate the Conduct of the War Department in the War with Spain.* 56th Cong., 1st ses., 1900. S. Doc. 221.

[21] Cosmas, *An Army For Empire,* 305.

[22] Ibid., 306.

[23] _____, *Military Reform,* 14.

[24] Ibid., 15.

[25] Ibid.

[26] U.S. Congress. Senate *Report Number 1671,* 55th Cong., 3rd Session (Washington D.C., 1899).

[27] Cosmas, *Military Reform,* 15. This is an interesting argument considering the mixed reviews of the current state militia forces.

[28] Ibid., 16

[29] Cosmas, *Military Reform,* 17.

[30] Linn, *The Philippine War,* 125.

CHAPTER 5

THE HISTORY OF THE THIRTY-SECOND INFANTRY REGIMENT, UNITED STATES VOLUNTEERS

> I _____ do hereby acknowledge to have voluntarily enlisted as a **SOLDIER** in the **VOLUNTEER ARMY OF THE UNITED STATES OF AMERICA** *[sic]* for the period ending June 30, 1901, unless sooner discharged by proper authority; and do also agree to accept from the United States such bounty, pay, rations, and clothing as are or may be established by law. And I do solemnly swear (or affirm) that I will bear true faith and allegiance to the United States of America, and that I will serve them honestly and faithfully against all their enemies whomsoever; and that I will obey the orders of the President of the United States and the orders of the officers appointed over me, according to the Rules and Articles of War.
>
> > Oath of Enlistment for members of the Volunteer Army of the Unites States[1]

Recruiting the Regiment

In March 1899, the Army Act solidified the concept, created the authorization, and provided the funding for federal volunteer regiments, but many of the important details related to this experiment had not been determined. It took the Office of the Adjutant General an additional four months to determine the exact organization, provide for the recruiting, procure the equipment and establish criteria for the appointment of officers to these regiments.[2]

Even if the details were not yet solidified, news of the pending growth in volunteer regiments spread quickly and excitement filled communities near army installations. The front page of the *Leavenworth Evening Standard* on 4 March 1899 proclaimed, "With the new army bill passed and [with the] the appropriations for Fort

Leavenworth, this post will be one of the most important military centers in the United States." The article followed, "the new army bill makes it almost assured that at least one of the volunteer regiments will be organized at Fort Leavenworth," and, "the Missouri valley is one of the best recruiting grounds in the United States."[3] The newspaper was correct on all counts.

A week later, Louis Aleck Craig was awarded the commission of "Colonel of Volunteers" by President McKinley and assigned as the commander of the 32nd Infantry Regiment, United States Volunteers.[4] The commanders of most of the volunteer regiments had previously held lower ranking regular commissions and Craig was no different. Previous to this promotion, he had been a regular army captain and served in both the Indian Wars and the Spanish-American War.

Colonel Craig was born in St. Joseph, Missouri, the son of a Congressman, Union General, and railroad tycoon.[5] He graduated from West Point in 1874 and served fifteen years with the "Old Army" on the frontiers of New Mexico and Arizona. For the great majority of his career, Craig served with the 6th Cavalry Regiment (most notable for its actions fighting in the Apache Wars) and at one point in the late 1870's he was among the officers who established the small frontier camp in Arizona known as Camp Huachuca.[6] Based on his frontier experience, I can be surmised that Colonel Craig was an experienced officer in irregular warfare.

In 1890, Craig was detailed to West Point to teach cavalry tactics, where he stayed for nearly a decade. In 1898 he was brevetted--awarded a temporary higher rank-- as a Major of Volunteers and posted to the staff of Major General Wilson in Puerto Rico, where he again saw combat.[7] It was after this posting that Colonel Craig was awarded command of the 32nd. When his regiment demobilized in 1901, Colonel Craig retired to

New York to recover from the malaria he contracted in the Philippines. He succumbed to

the disease in 1904 leaving behind his wife and two sons and a daughter. Both of his sons

would follow their father in service and rise into the general officer ranks--one would

lead a division and a corps against Germany in World War II, the other became the

fourteenth Chief of Staff of the Army.[8]

Photo Removed Due to Copyright Restrictions

Figure 5.   Colonel Louis A Craig, 32nd Infantry Regiment, U.S.V.
Source: Craig Family Archives

Other key senior officers of the 32nd Infantry included Lieutenant Colonel Lewis

H. Strother (Regimental Executive Officer) and Majors Robert E. L. Spence, Morton

Henry and Charles Cabell (Battalion Commanders). Among these officers, only Strother and Spence held regular army commissions (captain of the 22nd Infantry and first-lieutenant of the 16th Infantry, respectively), but all had previous combat experience with various state militia regiments.[9] While all of the senior officers were assigned prior to the start of recruiting for the regiment, most of the company grade officers were assigned or recruited along with the soldiers. These officers would be placed in command of companies and platoons only after Colonel Craig judged their abilities in training.

Photo Removed Due to Copyright Restrictions

Figure 6.   Lewis Strother at V.M.I., 1877
Source: Archives of the Virginia Military Institute, http://www.vmi.edu/archivephotos Details-aspACCNUM=2530&num=2331&rform=list (accessed 8 Feb 2006).

Lieutenant Colonel Strother was not only an excellent infantryman, he was also an experienced Indian fighter on the high plains. Strother graduated at the top of his class from the Virginia Military Institute (V.M.I.) in1877 (in the same class as George S. Patton, II) and immediately accepted a job as a professor at his alma mater. After several years of teaching, he joined the 1st Infantry Regiment and began his military career in earnest. In 1891, as a first lieutenant, he was recognized by the army for "highly efficient services while conducting a band of Cheyenne Indians from Pine Ridge, South Dakota, to Fort Keogh, Montana."[10] After this recognition, he was promoted to captain and offered command of a company. In early 1898 he was promoted to the rank of major and engineering officer in the 22nd Infantry Regiment (regulars), where he remained until the Philippine insurrection.[11]

Among the outstanding group of field grade officers in Craig's new command, Major Robert E. L. Spence may have been the most competent and accomplished, switching often between volunteer and regular units. Spence graduated from West Point in 1893 and served for five years with the 16th Infantry Regiment in Utah and Idaho. Spence deployed with the 16th Infantry to Cuba and was wounded in the attack on San Juan Hill. While he was recuperating in Georgia, Spence accepted a volunteer commission and deployed to Puerto Rico with the Georgia Volunteer Infantry. He quickly rose to the brevet rank of lieutenant colonel of volunteers in the fighting. Spence demobilized along with his men in April 1899 and returned to duties as a regular army lieutenant. By July of the same year, Spence had accepted a commission as a major of volunteers and the position of battalion commander in the Colonel Craig's 32nd Infantry Regiment, U.S.V..[12] When the 32nd returned to the United States in 1901, Spence remained in The Philippines as a major of regulars for an additional two years. He continued to serve the nation in and out of uniform for the next 20 years. Spence was elected state senator in Georgia in 1911 and he returned to the army once again as a lieutenant colonel in the 5th Infantry Regiment in World War I.[13] Major Spence is recognized as the American who officer first understood the military value the town of

Olongapo, on Subic Bay, and first secured it for American use. That land would serve as an essential American naval base in the Pacific for the next ninety-four years.[14]

Figure 7.   Major Spence as a Cadet in 1893.
Source: United States Military Academy Association of Graduates, *Register of Graduates and Former Cadets of the United States Military* (West Point, N.Y.: Association of Graduates, USMA, 1993).

By 16 July, when Colonel Craig arrived in Kansas, 8 officers and 154 recruits of the 32nd were already quartered at Fort Leavenworth. Recruits were arriving from all over the Midwest at a rate of about 25 new soldiers a day.[15] Craig intended for the regiment to be at full strength within a month, so he immediately sent all of his available officers on recruiting trips, each accompanied by two combat-experienced soldiers. By 20 July, *The Leavenworth Evening Standard* reported that recruiting had officially begun all around the Midwest. The newspaper indicated that recruiting stations existed in St. Louis, Des Moines, Omaha, Wichita, and Kansas City. From these stations, "recruiting parties [would] be sent out to the small towns, wherever there may be applicants of enlistment." The newspaper further added, "ex-soldiers will, of course, stand the best chance of getting non-commission officers warrants."[16] Although the exact destination of each of the recruiting teams cannot be determined, based on the recruit demographics, 32nd Infantry recruiters traveled as far as Colorado, the Dakotas, Oklahoma, and Indiana. The great majority of recruits, though, came from Missouri and Kansas.[17]

Volunteer recruits were required to be between the ages of eighteen and thirty-five years old, they were expected to be "of good character and habits, able-bodied, and free from disease," and unless specifically waived, recruits were to be at least five feet four inches and weigh between 120 and 190 pounds.[18] Men under twenty-one years old were required to obtain the written permission of their parents, as was the case with Private Karl D. White, the author of the most complete 32nd Infantry Regiment soldier's diary available today.[19] In light of the tropical hardships that awaited a new recruit, physical fitness was a critical element in the recruiting standards. The regulation went so far as to state, "In view of the probable severe service of these regiments and the climatic conditions to which they may be subjected, the physical qualifications of officers and enlisted men are of first importance."[20]

The noncommissioned officers in the regiment were generally soldiers with regular or Spanish-American War militia service who understood the drill regulations, could teach younger men and seemed to have the propensity for small unit leadership. Colonel Craig retained responsibility for promotions and reductions of non-commissioned officers in his regiment and it seems he understood the need for combat experienced men leading his soldiers. There are instances where a soldier without wartime experience was promoted into a leadership position, although this seems to be the exception. One such exception was Private Wirt Adams. Private Adams enlisted on 28 July 1899 in Kansas City, MO. His enlistment and training records indicate that he was only five feet-four inches tall; but what he lacked in size it seems Private Adams made up for in marksmanship and leadership ability. On the training range, Adams hit 86% of targets at 100 yards, 47% at 200 yards, 37% at 300 yards and 33% at 500 yards. Less than a month into his enlistment (before leaving Kansas), Adams was promoted to Corporal. While in the Philippines, Adams was further promoted up to the rank of Battalion Sergeant Major. In March 1901 (before returning to the United States), his Battalion Commander and Colonel Craig both endorsed his application for a regular army commission.[21]

At the beginning of organized recruiting (22 July), the 32nd Infantry reported an overall strength of 220 men.[22] When the Regimental strength reached 350 a short three days later, the first seven (of what would become twelve) companies were organized as "provisional company one" through "provisional company seven" with 50 men each.[23] Once recruited, a soldier was transported to Ft. Leavenworth where he was assigned to one of the provisional companies and organized under a non-commissioned officer for initial drill instruction, as well as the issuance of khaki uniforms and soldier kit. Most records indicate that uniforms and equipment arrived at the volunteer regiments quickly, but not always in a manner that could be accurately predicted. Therefore, at least initially, soldiers of the 32nd were issued whatever equipment was available. Then, as companies were formed, soldiers were issued the remainder of their uniforms, field gear, and the .308 caliber, Krag-Jorgenson rifle (colloquially referred to as the "Krag"). Praise for the accuracy, reliability, and lethality of this rifle is nearly universal in the literature of the time.[24] When fully manned and equipped, each numbered company was redesignated with its corresponding letter-"A Company" through "H Company."

The pace of recruiting for the 32nd Regiment was astounding. Just over two weeks after recruiting began, more than a thousand young men from around the midwest had enlisted and arrived in Kansas for service with the 32nd Regiment. There are surely many complicated and interconnected reasons for the success of this recruiting effort. Included among the reasons were: the sense of national service that continued to exist in the rural parts of the country even as it dissipated in the cities, the fact that a known expiration date was associated with enlistment in the Federal Volunteers, the prestige associated with joining a federal regiment, and the effective recruiting organization that Colonel Craig built.

Training the Regiment

With six weeks remaining before their scheduled departure, the 32nd left the comfortable barracks of Fort Leavenworth, marched a mile south and set-up their training camp, known as Camp Virginia. The camp was established on the same ground where the 21st Kansas Infantry Regiment prepared for war a year earlier.[25] (Since that time, Fort Leavenworth has expanded to encompass what was Camp Virginia, which existed on what is now the post's driving range.) The regiment continued to receive soldiers for the first few days of camp, but by 10 August Colonel Craig declared the regiment to be full. At 1609 men, the 32nd regiment was the third largest of the volunteer regiments and among the first regiments to be declared full.[26]

Photo Removed Due to Copyright Restrictions

Figure 8.   The 32nd Infantry at Camp Virginia, Leavenworth, KS, August 1899
Source: Craig Family Archives

Training in camp focused on marksmanship, physical fitness (mostly through long

marches) and open order tactics. The officers placed a particular emphasis on

marksmanship, probably based both on their experiences in combat and on orders from

higher army headquarters. This stress on marksmanship would continue throughout the

regiment's deployment.[27] Craig's soldiers trained for action at the small unit level often

and generally avoided regimental drills. Soldiers drilled in open order tactics that not only

emphasized aggressive pursuit of the enemy and the use of fire and maneuver, but it also

stressed fire control. This emphasis on both aggressiveness and restraint would serve the

regiment well from their first days in the Philippines.[28] The existence of written

soldiering manuals and books aided the development of the regiment's soldiers. Official

manuals included the *Infantry Drill Regulations of 1891* and *The Soldier's Handbook of

1898.* Other privately published books were written based on Cuba and Puerto Rico

experiences and, although they were not officially endorsed, it is quite probable they

were also used in tactical training.[29] The existence and use of such manuals seems to

indicate that the 32nd was not extraordinary in its training regimen; instead volunteer regiments across the country used the same manuals and therefore trained similarly. The differences in training probably lay in the quality of leadership, quality of training resources and equipment, and quality of solider recruited. In all of these areas, the 32nd excelled.

Soldiers of the 32nd most often practiced their maneuvers at the company level. A volunteer company consisted of three officers (a captain, a first lieutenant and a second lieutenant), six sergeants, twelve corporals, eighty-three privates, two cooks and an artificer (weapons expert). This emphasis on small unit leadership, allowed the company to organize itself in accordance with the tactical situation. A company could operate as a single unit or as an element in a higher organization, but most often, especially in the attack, it organized itself into firing, support and reserve platoons (each led by an officer).[30] Neither the company nor the regiment maintained any indirect fire or rapid-fire weaponry so the volunteer soldiers learned to mass their rifle fire accurately in order to provide cover for a maneuvering element. The emphasis on well-aimed fire and autonomous small unit maneuver would also serve the regiment well during counter-guerilla and occupation operations.

Colonel Craig, his officers and most of his non-commission officers had personal experience with the notoriously disease-ridden Spanish-American War mobilization camps. Based on this experience, the regiment placed great emphasis on sanitation, cleanliness and discipline while in camp. Those soldiers whose tents were not kept in perfect order usually heard directly from the commander.[31]

The regimental commander was a serious man, but he was not without a sense that soldiers needed time for relaxation and amusement. Seeking opportunities to provide his soldiers respite from the training regime, Colonel Craig recruited musicians working at the Soldiers' Home in Leavenworth to serve in the regimental band[32]. He also contracted with Anheuser-Busch brewery in Saint Louis to set up a canteen on the campsite.[33]

Photo Removed Due to Copyright Restrictions

Figure 9.   The 32nd Infantry Regiment Band
Source: Craig Family Archives

Over the next six weeks, the regiment completed all of their training on schedule and within the standards set out by Colonel Craig and the War Department. The intense schedule in the hot Kansas summer weeded out the weak, the unfit and the undisciplined. By mid-September, when they received order for deployment, the regimental strength had fallen to about 1300 soldiers.[34] On 16 September 1899, the 32nd Regiment departed Fort Leavenworth by train for Kansas City, Missouri. They paraded through the streets of Kansas City and were presented their regimental colors by a former Congressman and local judge, John F. Philips. By four o'clock that afternoon, the 32nd had re-boarded their trains and departed for San Francisco. [35]

Arriving in Oakland on 20 September, the soldiers of the 32nd made their way across the bay to the Presidio of San Francisco where the regiment waited for ships to take them to the Philippines. During their ten days in camp at the Presidio, the regiment, along with several other volunteer infantry regiments, received additional training in marksmanship, drill, and hiking. Because each regiment trained at their home-stations to a slightly different standard, this camp was specifically created to provide a uniform level of training to all deploying soldiers. It also served as a last opportunity for the leadership to remove soldiers who were physically incapable of service in the tropics. [36]

Photo Removed Due to Copyright Restrictions

Figure 10. The 32nd marches through Leavenworth to awaiting trains
September 16, 1899
Source: Craig Family Archives

On 30 September, three of the 32nd's companies marched through the streets of San Francisco to the docks at Fort Mason under the command of Major Spence. That afternoon, this lead element of the regiment joined the 33rd Infantry Regiment U.S.V. aboard the United States Army Transport Ship (U.S.A.T.) *Sheridan* and set sail. The next day, two troop carriers departed San Francisco carrying the rest of the 32nd. Most sailed aboard the U.S.A.T. *Glenogle* under Colonel Craig's command, while the two remaining companies (C and D) sailed an hour later on the U.S.A.T *Charles Nelson*.[37]

Figure 11. U.S.A.T. Glenogle
Source: Archives of the 32nd Infantry Regimental Association, Combined Arms Research Library, Fort Leavenworth, KS, Box 2.

About a week into their trip, all three ships stopped in Honolulu to refuel and refill the onboard stores. This brief break provided the soldiers of the 32nd an opportunity to stretch their legs and enjoy the dry land. Beautiful as it was, the sergeants of the 32nd did not let the opportunity for additional training pass. For each of the three days in Honolulu, soldiers conducted marching, open order drill, and manual-of-arms or shooting exercises.[38] The regiment arrived in the Philippines on 17 October, 29 October and 1 November after less than three months in existence.[39]

In light of the 32nd's record thus far, it must be concluded that the regiment was well recruited, well trained, and well led. The focus that Colonel Craig and his officers placed on physical fitness, marksmanship, open order drill, and discipline created an organization that was fully prepared to take on the physical rigor and mental ambiguity of a counterinsurgency fight. Within days of its arrival, the 32nd soldiers would be given the opportunity to test themselves against Aguinaldo's army.

Combat Operations

In order to characterize the success of the 32nd it is important to review a cross section of its actions. Accordingly, the next section discusses several different combat actions, each taking place at different times in the deployment and under varying circumstances. It would be a mistake to surmise that no active combat took place during the "nation-building" operations or no civic development was attempted at the same time combat was at its peak. In fact, it is the ability to conduct both tasks simultaneously that marked the volunteer regiments as outstanding units. While building civil capacity and infrastructure occurred through out their deployment, the majority of the 32nd Infantry's active combat operations occurred during the first half of their eighteen months in the Philippines. It was during this timeframe that American forces mounted their strongest attacks against the Philippine Army of Liberation (P.A.L), destroyed it as a viable conventional adversary and then refocused to fight an aggressive counterinsurgency war.

The arrival of volunteer regiments like the 32nd Infantry in late October, 1899 completed General Otis' preparations for the northern offensive. He hoped the arriving

63

newly formed regiments would give the American army the operational strength and the fresh legs required to bring decisive strategic victory in the Philippines. Therefore, almost immediately upon disembarking their ships, the 32nd boarded trains to join the ongoing fight at the northern limit of American advance--the town of Angeles.[40] As Colonel Craig reported to his new commander, Major General Arthur MacArthur, the regiment made camp and drew one hundred rounds of ammunition and two days rations per soldier.[41] Because the 32nd was still waiting for two of its companies (U.S.A.T. *Charles Nelson* had not yet arrived), it was assigned the task of guarding the town of Angeles and the rail line that ran through it.[42] While on their outposts, the 32nd soldiers faced harassment fires and probing attacks, but their training allowed them to discriminate between harassment and a direct attack. Without firing a shot, the nervous soldiers of the 32nd held their ground for five nights. In his report to the Secretary of War, Colonel Craig reported, "the 32nd began outpost duty and for five days and nights it faced an active and annoying enemy without firing a shot thereby making an exceptional record."[43]

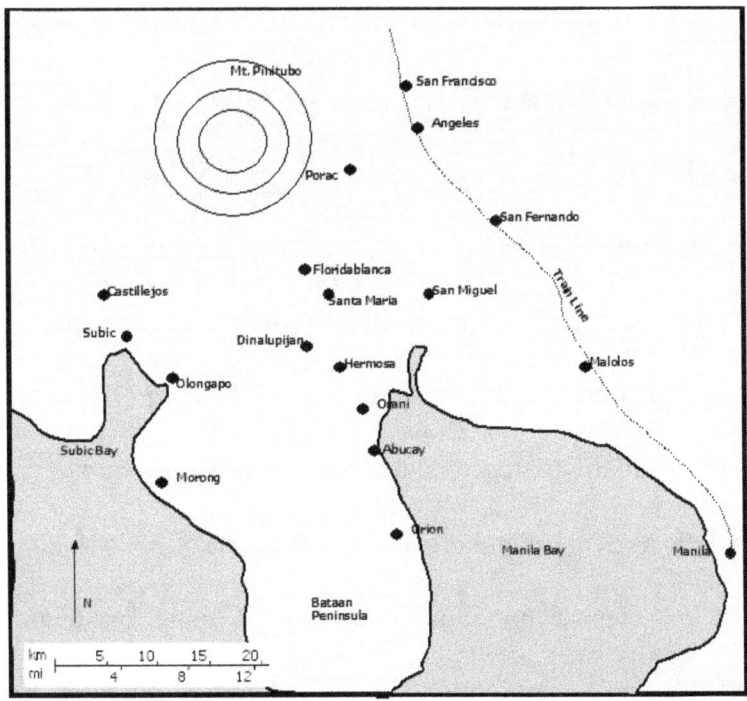

Figure 12. The 32nd's Area of Operations in Central Luzon

New orders came early on 5 November and at 5 a.m. three companies of the regiment marched north in support MacArthur's attempt to fix the Filipino army. The 32nd soldiers marched nearly twelve miles as a reserve force while protecting the supply lines and train tracks. At the front (often less than 200 yards away), the 17th Infantry (regulars) dislodged the Filipino army town by town. Private White recalled bullets flying overhead and heavy firing ahead, but he most notably remembered the action as "wallowing along in mud and water, sometimes waist deep" until 2 a.m. the next day.[44]

When the last two companies joined the regiment at Angeles, further orders soon followed. The 32nd was reassigned to Brigadier General F.D. Grant's brigade it was immediately ordered to relieve a besieged patrol of American scouts north of Angeles.[45] The small patrol was completely cut off from friendly lines. It was under heavy fire and in danger of being overrun. Captain Granville Sevier, the E Company commander, led the rescue mission. Sevier and his soldiers fought their way up to besieged scouts and found that they had stumbled into a series of well-organized trench works. Although the fire was heavy, Captain Sevier quickly realized that it was not accurate and he led an open-order attack on the positions. The Filipinos were overwhelmed by the speed of 32nd attack and were pushed back behind their third line of works, over 500 yards to the rear.[46] This action not only rescued the besieged patrol, but it routed a deliberate P.A.L. attack as well. Because of their aggressive and organized action, the 32nd took no casualties during this attack, its first major action in the Philippines. Colonel Craig later recommended Captain Sevier for promotion to brevet-major of volunteers for his "courage and coolness in command" of this relief mission.[47]

By the end of November, MacArthur was confident enough in the success of his portion of the northern campaign that he wrote to Otis, "The so-called Filipino Republic is destroyed. The Congress has dissolved. The President of the so-called republic is a fugitive...The [Filipino] army as an organization has disappeared."[48] MacArthur argued in favor of an amnesty for Filipino soldiers and civil penalties for officers who continued to pursue war against the Americans. Otis disagreed. He argued that the Philippine Army of Liberation was still strong in the southern islands and in the Bataan Peninsula and that the time was not right for amnesty.[49] In this case at least, Otis was correct. Even if the P.A.L. was near ruin, the Bataan Province remained a stronghold for resistance activities. MacArthur decided that it was essential to remove this source of Filipino strength if his amnesty ideas were going to gain acceptance with headquarters in Manila.

In early December 1899, the 32nd regiment received the mission to clear Bataan of resistance.[50] Colonel Craig, whose companies were stationed in the key towns and villages stretching from Angeles (in the north) down to Floridablanca (in the south), alerted his units for action. On 1 December, Colonel Craig led a movement of several companies from San Fernando towards Floridablanca, a town at the northern limit of the Bataan Province. At around 5 p.m. on 2 December, Colonel Craig's column was fired upon and a brief firefight ensued. The aggressive action and accuracy of the American column quickly overpowered the Filipino ambush and killing 20 men and dispersing the rest. In the action, the American's killed a Filipino captain who was found wearing the engraved sword and revolver of Ensign H.C. Wood, U. S. Navy. This naval officer had been killed on his gunboat four months earlier in a Filipino river ambush.[51]

The soldiers of the 32nd spent their days on patrols and their nights in makeshift shelters and unfinished buildings as the remainder of Grant's Brigade fought their way to Floridablanca.[52] On 5 December, Grant's brigade was complete and he pushed his attack into Bataan Province for what would become a near constant battle for two weeks. In the first significant action of this campaign, Major Spence led a patrol of one hundred men across extremely difficult terrain to link up with Navy forces that were headed to Subic Bay. On the 9 December, after skirmishing nearly the entire distance (approximately 15 mountainous miles), Spence and his patrol seized the town of Olongapo and with it a P.A.L. naval station and a resupply base.[53] When the Navy arrived by ship the next day and took control of the facility, Spence and his patrol marched north to clear the rest of Subic Bay. Spence's patrol drove the insurgents out of the town of Subic where they captured two hundred rounds of ammunition. Spence allowed his patrol to rest for a day in Subic and then the column marched 10 more miles north and pushed the Filipino army out of Castillejos. All over Bataan, similar activities occurred at a similar pace. Company sized patrols of American soldiers entered small towns and systematically ejected the P.A.L. from its resource base.[54] By the end of December, the Philippine Army of Liberation was no longer a viable conventional military force in Bataan.

District Life

Between 10 and 20 January, the 32nd Regimental headquarters and those companies that were garrisoning towns in central Luzon moved closer to Bataan. As conventional military activities ended, the most relevant tactic in the pacification of the Philippines became occupation rather than pursuit. The tactical brigade command structure transformed itself into administrative departments and district commands. The garrisons established during this period would last, with few changes, until the regiment redeployed in March of 1901. The 32nd Regiment, now assigned to the 5th District, Department of Northern Luzon, established a line of garrisons that stretched nearly 100 miles from Angeles, Pampanga down to the southern tip of the Bataan Peninsula. Even by today's standards, this is an astounding amount of territory for twelve companies of lightly armed soldiers.

Photo Removed Due to Copyright Restrictions

Figure 13. The 32nd Regiment headquarters building, Orani, Bataan Province
Source: Craig Family Archives

As the companies of the 32nd settled into semi-autonomous district life,
skirmishes with the insurgents continued, especially in those towns closest to the
mountains. One such town was Porac, which was due west of Angeles, nestled on the
lower slopes of Mount Pinatubo. The young leaders of the 32nd recognized that the
insurgents were using the difficult mountainous country to base their guerilla operations
and hide their supplies, so they concentrated their patrolling in these areas. On 13 June
1900, Lieutenant Mapes and 15 men from M Company were taking part in what had
become a standard "hike" between towns when they surprised a small band of insurgents.
The enemy fled and was not found, but the direction of their flight led the Americans to a
huge guerilla cache.[55] The find was important enough to be included in the army's annual
report to the Secretary of War. MacArthur, now commander of all Philippine based
activities, reported, "Lieutenant Mapes…captured 1,000 pounds of powder, 200 cannon
balls, 150 1-pound shells (Hotchkiss), 20 13-pound shells, 10 6-inch shells, 100 pounds

of dynamite, 20,000 mauser shells and clips, 50 gallons of chemicals, and 1 mauser cartridge machine complete."[56] On 10 August, another M Company patrol found another huge stash. In this instance, M Company secured 700 rounds of rapid-fire ammunition, 100 rounds of grape shot, 300 hand grenades and 10,000 round of Remington ammunition.[57] The loss of such a substantial amount of supplies undoubtedly hindered insurgent activities in the region and allowed the regiment to concentrate more closely on "benevolent assimilation" of the Filipino population rather than on warfare with the insurgents.

Figure 14. A Patrol from G Co, 32nd Infantry U.S.V. is ambushed between Dinalupijan and Hermosa, 19 February 1900.
Source: Archives of the 32nd Infantry Regimental Association

Because most of the action took place at the company level or lower, it is not possible to count the number of skirmishes, patrols, deliberate attacks and defenses that the 32nd undertook in their time in the Philippines. There are, however, records to indicate that these soldiers were in near-constant struggles. For example, the regimental scouts documented at least twenty-six distinct skirmishes from June 1900 through March 1901--these were "the calm" months.[58] Colonel Craig's report to the Secretary of War, which only lists those actions that rise to the level worthy of reporting back to Washington, records an average of four or five actions per week. At this rate of activity, there can be no question that the 32nd was successfully pursuing the Filipino insurgents throughout their deployment. However, the true measure of the success of the 32nd would be measured not by insurgents killed, but by elections held, children taught and local governments organized.

Civil Operations

The 32nd experience in the Philippines was as a lightly armed counterinsurgency force. Their primary tactic to accomplish pacification of the Filipino people was to occupy the small towns, demonstrate through (civic and structural improvements) the potential of American rule and limit the ability for the insurgents to influence the Filipino population. In this task, the 32nd was successful. Usually separated from any command higher than their own company, the soldiers developed and affinity for their towns and for Filipino people among whom they lived. For the most part, the regiment's soldiers maintained an amicable, if not friendly, relationship with the populace and in doing so they were able to recognize and limit insurgent influence while at the same time building essential civic capacity at the lowest levels

The concept of the American army managing civil administration in the Philippines was not new when the 32nd arrived. McKinley's use of the term benevolent assimilation in 1898 implied as much, but pacifying the Filipino population was not a simple occupation task, even after the destruction of Aquinaldo's Philippine Army of

Liberation. The officers and soldiers of the 32nd had to quickly develop plans for schools, elections, infrastructure repairs, policing and many other tasks associated with civil governance. It was not an easy transition, but the 32nd proved to be an exceptionally capable organization for civil administration.

In 1898, when American forces occupied Manila and nothing else, General Otis spoke of bringing the Filipino people "good government" in exchange for recognizing the "complete and unquestioned" sovereignty of the United States.[59] But while Otis was issuing proclamations from Manila, Aguinaldo was building governmental structures in the rest of the country. These shadow governments filled the vacuum that was created when the Spanish authorities left. The arrival of the volunteer regiments in the fall of 1899 gave the United States Army in the Philippines enough strength to venture beyond the walled city of Manila, to actually occupy towns and villages, and to begin the pacification and assimilation of the Filipino people in earnest. The army became the primary instrument by which the United States intended to end the guerilla war and prepare the Philippines for colonial government. In preparation for colonial government, President McKinley established the "Philippine Commission" (headed by William H. Taft) in March 1900 to supervise the transfer of authority from the army to civilian government, province by province.

The 32nd Regiment's civic operations were governed by two key documents. General Order Number 43 (issued by Otis in his capacity as the Commander of the Eight Army Corps on 8 August 1899) and General Order Number 40 (issued by Otis in his later capacity as the Military Governor of the Philippine Islands on 29 March 1900). G.O. 43 limited its focus to security and stability near Manila and Luzon's essential piece of infrastructure, the railway. It required those military commanders who occupied towns along the Luzon Railway to establish temporary civil governments. Further, those commanders who occupied towns removed from the rail line were encouraged to establish governments where "civil administration is wanting."[60] Among the specific requirements, G.O. 43 tasked commanders to establish elections for municipal councils and town presidents, establish police forces, enforce sanitary measures, to establish schools and establish and regulate markets.[61] Six months later, G.O. 40 expanded the scope of civil requirements and further defined the roles of the municipal councils and mayors, known as *alcaldes*. It established regulations for elections, taxation, finances, and it went as far as to specify the salary and oath of office for each elected or appointed position. Most importantly, G.O. 40 required the U.S. officers to regularly report to Manila the status of civil institutions in the town they occupied.[62] However, the General Order remained unspecific in relation to how to accomplish each task, so the volunteer officers were pushed to think critically about their specific situations and act according to their regional knowledge and instincts. They did not apply a one-size-fits-all approach. Governor Taft implied as much when he reported to the Secretary of War, "the pacification of the islands seems to depend largely on the character of the military officer in charge of the particular district."[63]

In the small towns that served as garrisons for the 32nd, the soldiers did not seem to make a clear distinction between their civil duties and their military duties. To these men it was all the duty of a soldier. In the four months between December 1899 and March 1900 the 32nd occupied and established civil governments in fourteen different townships.[64] In his diary, Private Karl White wrote extensively about serving on guard duty, conducting patrols in search of insurgents or their caches, hiring and managing the work of local laborers, and establishing and working in the local schools. Often in the same entry, White references both civil and military operations; on 22 October 1900, White writes about going to the target range to complete his weapons qualifications, about getting in a "scrap" with the insurgents, and about the establishment of schools for both boys and girls (with free books provided by the American authorities).[65] It was at these schools that the soldiers most closely interacted with the population.

Figure 15.   Private Karl D. White, "at home" in Dinalupijan, Philippines
Source: Archives of the 32nd Infantry Regimental Association

Building Schools

Building schools and providing education to the populace were among the most important aspects of the local pacification policies. In nearly every town, schools were established and often, at least early in the process, soldiers were the teachers. In their capacity as provincial governors, regimental commanders were required to submit detailed monthly reports about the progress of education in their region. The August 1900

74

report submitted by Colonel Craig indicated that the 32nd had established twenty-five schools in sixteen different towns. In those schools, there were twenty-seven teacher and 888 students (550 boys and 338 girls). The subjects taught included English, Spanish, arithmetic, geography, United States history, hygiene, and Catholicism. Although not all subjects were taught in all schools, it seems that nearly every student at this time was learning Spanish. Also widespread was the teaching of Catholicism. It can be assumed that Midwestern farmers turned volunteer soldier were generally not teaching Catholicism; instead, the security provided by the Americans gave priests and missionaries new license to spread their faith. Finally, in his report to Manila, Colonel Craig indicated that nine of his schools had no books and six of them had no dedicated building. [66] The volunteer soldiers of the 32nd were teaching Filipino children in the open without the benefit of texts.

Figure 16. Privates Killingsworth, Bridges and Jordan (G Company) working on a construction project.
Source: Archives of the 32nd Infantry Regimental Association.

In December of the same year the number of schools had not changed, but the total number of students in school had nearly doubled to 1403 (846 boys and 557 girls). In another important evolution, over 90% of those students were now studying English as well as Spanish. The second most prevalent course was still Catholicism, but nearly 400 students were now learning arithmetic, four times the amount that were learning it three months earlier. The kind of needs reported by the schools changed over those three months, too. Requests evolved from the basics like books and buildings, to more advanced needs like desks, blackboards, maps, charts, and lesson plans for technical classes like geography and United States history. In the case of Captain Brandt's school in the town of Abucay, enrollment improved from almost nothing to nearly 200 in three months. Enrollment grew so fast in Abucay that by the end of 1900, Colonel Craig had requested authority to build an additional facility to teach girls and boys separately.[67]

Around the time the district system came into effect, Captain Henry Peed, the commander of C Company was designated as the Superintendent of Public Schools for the 5th District, Department of Northern Luzon. In this capacity, he reported through Colonel Craig to General Grant the status and plans for the education of the Filipino children. Typical of the emphasis that the regiment placed on education in the towns, the Superintendent of Public Schools held power beyond his rank. In one incident that occurred in March 1901, soldiers of the 6th Artillery Regiment were moving in to replace the 32nd Infantry soldiers in the town of Orion. During their occupation, the 6th recognized the most defensible and centrally located building and chose it as their headquarters. This building happened to be home to the local school. Captain Peed, in his capacity as the Superintendent of Schools was traveling between towns monitoring academic activities when noticed that the new unit had taken for itself what was the town's school-house. In his report to General Grant, Captain Peed recommended that the eighty American soldiers be evicted from their quarters and the school be reinstated. The commander of the 6th Artillery rebutted that the building was not only in the best tactical position, but that it was originally built as a barracks and should be used as such. In the end, Captain Peed won the argument with the regimental commander and the 6th Artillery camped (presumably in their tents, during the rainy season) while the children of Orion reoccupied the former barracks as their school.[68]

Elections

Another very important aspect to the 32nd pacification efforts was the implementation of democratic reforms: specifically the election of local leaders. G.O. 40 stated that "the Philippine people are to exercise the right of suffrage in the election of municipal officers--a right only slightly restricted by conditions which have been imposed for the purpose of rewarding as well as encouraging the people in their just and natural aspirations."[69] Although not directly stated, in practice the order required each occupied town to have an American officer act as its mayor until that officer certified the town free enough from insurgent control hold a legitimate election. Although there seems to have been pressure to hold elections as soon as possible, officers in the towns we able to deflect this pressure and used their knowledge of local conditions to make their recommendations. Although local elections had been held under the watchful eye of the army in many towns (especially those towns close to Manila) for almost a year, as late as August 1900 Lieutenant Colonel Strother reported that the towns under his control in the Balanga Province were still not "ready to receive the benefits of G.O. 40."[70] It seems from these reports that the officers of the 32nd took their responsibilities of advising, building and monitoring the civic development of the Filipino's very seriously.

An incident which took place in the town of Macabebe in September of 1900 highlighted the dedication to rule of law that underpinned the 32nd soldiers as they executed their civic tasks. The citizens of Macabebe, because they had historically resisted Spanish rule and believed they would be second-class citizens in an Aguinaldo led government, were early supporters of the American occupation. The town held initial elections as early as August 1899 and it became famous for contributing militia units to integrate into the American counterinsurgency efforts--the "Macabebe Scouts." The September 1900 elections in Macabebe, monitored by Lieutenant George Densmore (H Company), seemed to run as planned and a young man by the name of Marcellino Bustos was declared the winner for the position of *second alcalde* (deputy mayor) by a vote of 153 to 129. However, after the fact, the election judges learned that Bustos was not yet twenty-six years old, the statutory age required for the position. Learning that the election may be declared invalid, Bustos typed a letter to the judge of provincial elections arguing that he was, in fact, of the required age but he could not produce a legal certificate of birth because it was destroyed in a church fire. [71] Bustos further bolstered his case by submitting a petition in his favor signed by thirty-six well-respected voters. In his report about the incident, Densmore wrote to Colonel Craig that he was "positive that [Bustos] is not more that twenty-two." Densmore continued, "but he is, in my opinion, the most capable young man in the town and would dignify the office."[72] After praising the attributes of the young man who was elected, Lieutenant Densmore returned his focus to the regulations. "Respect for orders must be instilled," he wrote, "the slip-shod manner in which these people have run their election will continue if this election is to be permitted." In his final argument to overturn the election, Densmore wrote, "I would suggest that they [the Macabebe people] be given their first lesson and made to understand that G.O. 40 means [*sic*] the letter of what it says."[73]

It is not known whether Bustos was removed from his position, but even if he was not, Densmore's position likely caused political difficulty in the town where he and his platoon lived. However, it is a testament to the respect for the rule of law and the belief in the adherence to regulations of the volunteer soldiers, that a junior officer like Lieutenant Densmore, would even consider taking such an locally unfavorable stand.

Election irregularities like the one detailed above were the exception rather than the rule. In Floridablanca, Captain Frank Eckers (I company) monitored the September 1900 elections and reported back that the local election commissioners not only counted votes, but also followed up with those who registered to vote but failed to do so. They determined that the great majority of the non-voters were sick. Eckers reported that the high turnout and the diverse pool of men who received votes was "the best evidence that…no undue influence was used."[74]

For the last six months of their tour, life for the soldiers of the 32nd settled into a rotation of outpost guard duty, garrison duty (including infrastructure repair, teaching school, and interacting with the population), and patrolling to keep insurgents on the run The accomplishments of the 32nd Infantry are even more amazing when considered along with the physical toll the Philippine environment placed on these Midwestern men. By the time the 32nd mustered out of service, it had experienced the deaths of 50 men, only 13 of whom died from direct contact with an enemy. As they did in their Kansas camp, the regimental leadership placed a high emphasis on cleanliness and sanitation in their Filipino garrisons, but the climate proved to be formidable. During their tenure in the tropics, 171 soldiers became sick enough to be sent back to the United States for treatment. [75] At nearly every point in their deployment one quarter of the 32nd soldiers were on the sick roles and six officers, including Colonel Craig, were granted leave from the Philippines in order to recuperate from their tropical diseases.[76] Colonel Craig never fully recovered and he died of malarial complications, less than three years after returning to the United States.

Between 15 and 22 March 1901, the 32nd moved to Camp Wallace, on the outskirts of Manila to prepare for the return trip to the United States. On 22 March, having been in the Philippines for seventeen months, they conducted a review for General MacArthur, said their farewells to those officers and soldiers who had volunteered to stay, and boarded the U.S.A.T. *Grant.*[77] As the *Grant* steamed out of Manila Bay on the afternoon of 23 March, it passed the U.S.A.T. *Sheridan,* carrying the fresh soldiers from the newly formed 21st and 27th Regular Infantry Regiments.[78] The short-lived primacy of Federal Volunteer Regiments in the American military system was slowly coming to a close.

---

[1] CMSR, 32nd Infantry Regiment (U.S.V).

[2] The official orders for the mobilization of these regiments came four months later in the form of General Order No. 122 on 5 July 1899.

[3] LES, 4 March 1899, 1.

[4] *Special Order No. 163* (Washington D.C.: Office of the Adjutant General of the Army, 13 July 1899).

[5] Ezra J Warner, *Generals in Blue: Lives of the Union Commanders* (Baton Rouge, LA: Louisiana State University Press, 1964) p 98-99. His father, Congressman James Craig served for two terms (1856-1860), before casting his support behind the presidency of Abraham Lincoln. As a "Lincoln-Democrat" in a slave state, he failed his nomination bid for a third term. In 1864 Lincoln commissioned him a general in the Union army and he spent the Civil War protected the western mail routes that originated in eastern Kansas.

[6] The History of Fort Huachuca, http://huachuca-www.army.mil/HISTORY/huachuca.htm (accessed on 4 Feb 06). This camp has grown to be the largest military installation in Arizona and the "Home of Military Intelligence"

[7] ANJ, Vol 41, No 30 (26 March 1904): 780-1.

[8] William Gardner Bell, *Commanding Generals and Chiefs of Staff* (Washington D.C: Center of Military History, 1983), 118.

[9] Roster of the 32nd Infantry U.S.V. (Balanga, Bataan Province, Philippine Islands: 32nd Regimental Headquarters, 1902). 31. This book can be found in the rare books collection, Combined Arms Research Library, Ft Leavenworth, KS.

[10] Theophilus F. Roddenbough, ed. *The Army of the United States: Historical Sketches of Staff and Line with Portraits of Generals-in-Chief* (New York: Maynard, Merrill and Company, 1896) 413. This book can be found on the World Wide Web at http://www.army.mil/cmh/books/R&H/R&H-1IN.htm (accessed 15 Feb 2006).

[11] Roster, 89.

[12] Although it cannot be proven from historical records, one can surmise that Craig and Spence knew each other from the Puerto Rico experience and Colonel Craig "pulled" this promising young officer into his regiment.

[13] United States Military Academy Association of Graduates, *Register of Graduates and Former Cadets of the United States Military Academy*. (West Point, NY: Association of Graduates, USMA, 48th ed., 1993), 831.

[14] Subic Bay Metropolitan Authority, http://www.lakbay.net/destinations/sbma/aboutus.asp (accessed on January 26 2006).

[15] LES, 17 July 1899, 3.

[16] LES, 20 July 1899, 3.

[17] Roster, 31-71.

[18] *Annual Report of the War Department 1899*, (Washington D.C.: Government Printing Office) Vol. 1, part 5, 66-8.

[19] CMSR, 32nd Infantry Regiment (U.S.V.).

[20] *Annual Report of the War Department 1899*, (Washington D.C.: Government Printing Office) Vol. 1, part 5, 67.

[21] Ibid.

[22] ANJ, Vol. 26, No. 47 (22 July 1899): 1120.

[23] Roster, 3.

[24] ANJ, Vol. 27, No. 49 (August 4, 1900): 1166.

[25] The 21st Kansas, unlike its famous sister regiment, the 20th, never saw action. It was designated to fight the Spanish in Puerto Rico and it trained at Leavenworth. The Regiment moved east in search of action, but the war ended before it could make through further training in Chattanooga Tennessee.

[26] LES, August 10, 1899, 4.

[27] RSW, 10.

[28] RSW, 12. Colonel Craig reported that, "On November 3rd the 32nd began outpost duty and for five days and nights it faced an active and annoying enemy without firing a shot thereby making an exceptional record."

[29] Other books include Arthur Wagner's *Catechisms of Outpost Duty* (1895), William Sprigind's *Catechismal Edition of Infantry Drill Regulations: Extended Order* (1898), and Melvin Rowell's *Private's Handbook of Military Courtesy and Guard Duty* (1898).

[30] U.S. War Department, *Infantry Drill Regulation, Extended Order Drill* (Washington D.C.: War Department, 1898), 15-6.

[31] LES, August 10 1899, 4.

[32] Created by Congress in 1851, Soldiers' Homes existed in many parts of the country to service the needs of elderly and disabled veterans (initially from the Mexican War). The Leavenworth Soldier's home existed on the site that now houses the federal VA hospital.

[33] LES, August 10 1899, 4.

[34] LES September 16 1899, 5.

[35] Ibid.

[36] ANJ, Vol. 27, No. 9 (October 27 1899): 190.

[37] RSW, 10.

[38] Roster, 5.

[39] RSW, 12.

[40] KDW, 1 November 1899.

[41] RSW, 10.

[42] William Thaddeus Sexton, *Soldiers in the Sun: An Adventure in Imperialism* (Freeport, NY: book for Libraries Press, 1939), 194.

[43] RSW, 12.

[44] KDW, 5 November 1899.

[45] Grant was the son of civil war hero and former U.S. President, General Ulysses S. Grant

[46] RSW, 12.

[47] Ibid., 38.

[48] Sexton, 198.

[49] Ibid.

[50] Under MacArthur's 2nd Division (which included Grant's Brigade, and Craig's Regiment), each regiment was given responsibility for security and operations in a large area (later to become the District system). At his time, the 32nd's assignment was the area that included most of the northern banks of Manila Bay including the northern parts of the Bataan Province.

[51] *Correspondence Relating to Movements of Columns in Zambales and Bataan*, NARA RG 395, E2702, Box 1.

[52] KDW, 3 Dec 1899.

[53] RSW, 13.

[54] Ibid., 13-15.

[55] Ibid.

[56] Nelson, A Miles, *Annual Report of the Lieutenant General Commanding the Army, 1900 (Washington, D.C: Government Printing Office 1901) 35.* (This reference is

embedded inside the *History of the Philippine Insurrection [microfilm] against the United States, 1899-1901* from the NARA)

[57] Ibid., 42.

[58] Charles Killingsworth, *Diary of Charles Killingsworth, Regimental Scouts, 32nd Infantry Regiment, United States Volunteers* (Fort Leavenworth, KS: Archives of the 32nd Infantry Regimental Association).

[59] Linn, *The U.S. Army and Counterinsurgency*, 11.

[60] U.S. Senate, *Hearings on Affairs on the Philippine Islands* (Washington D.C.: GPO, 1904), 127.

[61] Ibid.

[62] Ibid., 111.

[63] Linn, *The U.S. Army and Counterinsurgency*, 22. (Further attributed to W.H. Taft Papers, series vol. 21.)

[64] RSW, 27.

[65] KDW, 22 October 1900.

[66] Louis A. Craig, *Consolidated Report of Schools for the Month of August 1900 in Territory Occupied by the 32nd Infantry U.S.V.* Reports of Schools: 5th District Department of Northern Luzon, NARA, RG395, E2303.

[67] Louis A. Craig, *Consolidated Report of Schools for the Month of December 1900 in Territory Occupied by the 32nd Infantry U.S.V.* Reports of Schools: 5th District Department of Northern Luzon, NARA, RG395, E2303.

[68] Henry Peed, *Report that the only school in Orion is occupied by American Troops*, 30 March 1901, 5th District, Department of Northern Luzon, NARA RG 395 E. 2092 Box 2.

[69] *Hearings on Affairs on the Philippine Islands,* 112.

[70] Lewis Strother, *Telegram: Strother to Craig, 5 August 1900*, 5th District, Department of Northern Luzon, NARA RG 395 E. 2092.

[71] Marcellino Bustos, *Letter from Bustos to Judge of Elections,* 15 September 1900, Department of Northern Luzon, 5th District, NARA RG 395 E. 2092.

[72] George A. Densmore, *Letter from Densmore to Craig,* 17 September 1900, 5th District, Department of Northern Luzon, NARA RG 395 E. 2092.

[73] Ibid.

[74] Frank W. Eckers, *Letter from Eckers to Craig, 18 September 1900*, Department of Northern Luzon, 5th District, NARA RG 395 E. 2092.

[75] RSW, 28.

[76] Roster, 84.

[77] RSW, 37. Twenty-three officers remained in the Philippines, including: Lieutenant Colonel Strother and Major Spence with headquarters in the Manila, Captain Peed as Superintendent of Schools, Captain Goldman as the Military Governor of Bataan, Captain Eckers with the as an advisor to the native police, and Lieutenants Densmore, Ryan and Boyle leading companies of native troops.

[78] KDW, 23 March 1901.

CHAPTER 6

CONCLUSIONS

> Progress in the hoped-for direction has been favorable. Our forces have successfully controlled the greater part of the islands, overcoming the organized forces of the insurgents and carrying order and administrative regularity to all quarters. What opposition remains is for the most part scattered, obeying no concerted plan of strategic action. [1]
>
> President William McKinley, 3 December 1900

Through the history of a single unit, this thesis studied the issues that led to the creation of federal volunteer regiments during the Philippine Insurrection and the experiences of one of those regiments in active combat and counterinsurgency. Although caution must be taken when applying lessons from a single regiment to greater organizations or events, there are some general judgments about the 32nd that may enhance our understanding of the use of volunteers in counterinsurgency operations. First, the creation of federal volunteer forces demonstrated the efficacy of democratic political processes to provide military forces that met the needs of the citizenry, the politicians, and the generals. Second, the 32nd was a capable combat force, an effective counterinsurgency force, and it transitioned easily between the two types of operations. Finally, although the concept needs further study, the success of the 32nd Infantry Regiment in the Philippines may provide important lessons about organizing, manning, training, and fighting a counterinsurgency.

The volunteer regiments were the product of intense political negotiation and infighting at the highest levels of the United States military establishment. The army realized that the regular force was too small for its rapidly multiplying tasks. It looked to

86

expand and it struggled to replace the militia system with a military reserve system that produced more predictable and effective results. At the same time, militia leaders fought to ensure state relevance in any new national defense system. They wanted to contain the expansion of the regular army by designing a military reserve system that forced the nation to remain reliant on state soldiers as the national strategic reserve. Congress wanted to increase the number of soldiers in uniform, but feared that an increase in the regular force would be prohibitively expensive and it might be construed as approval for the McKinley administration's imperialist policies.

In the midst of this struggle, the United States acquired the Philippine Islands. America needed soldiers immediately to police its new empire, but the enlistments of the state militia units in the Philippine Islands were expired. Over three contentious months (including a rare third session) Congress arrived at a politically acceptable solution. The Army Act of 1899 was legislative "sausage-making" at its finest. No side was completely happy, but nearly everyone supported the compromise. By organizing volunteers directly under federal control, the President hoped to avoid the political and practical problems that he had experienced with previous call-ups of state militia units. By limiting the terms of the volunteers, the anti-imperialist Congress increased the uniformed force without increasing the size of the standing army. Finally, because this new force would be ready for deployment by October 1899, the military leaders in the Philippines could plan for new units to replace the state militiamen whose commitments had expired

The volunteer regiments combined the leadership quality that resided in the regular army with the motivation, spirit and determination of the militia units. The 32nd was a well-trained, well-led and capable infantry force that transitioned easily between conventional and counterinsurgency operations. In less than eighteen months, the 32nd destroyed Filipino conventional resistance in its assigned sector, severely degraded the guerilla resistance, pacified an amazingly large area of land, and created the civil structures that enabled the peace to last.

Most of the 32nd's officers had combat experience, but almost none had experienced the difficult combination of civil and military tasks that a counterinsurgency required. Nonetheless, the regiment was remarkably competent in the counterinsurgency. Officers led combat patrols aggressively and, when directed, they adapted their perspectives for occupation duty with similar savvy. The regimental focus on marksmanship training and open-order tactics proved its value from the first days in combat. Within a few months, the 32nd was able to push the Filipino conventional threat into the hills away from the population. The regiment kept the insurgents on the run while, at the same time, it instituted social and political reforms in the towns. The most crucial component of the 32nd success in the Philippines was its detailed attention to civic reforms--a task that fell not only to the officers, but also to the soldiers. Where the officers led, the soldiers followed. In most cases, the soldiers of the 32nd endured difficult conditions and ambiguous missions without resorting to the brutality that has been ascribed to the predecessor state militia units. The breadth of interactions that soldiers had with the locals through teaching school, organizing civil institutions and building infrastructure attests to the dedication of the 32nd soldiers to this task.

The success of the 32nd Infantry Regiment may also teach us some important lessons about manning, training, and fighting a counterinsurgency force. The 32nd was organized for a specific purpose, to fight and win the counterinsurgency in the

Philippines. It was comprised of volunteer soldiers recruited mostly from the farm fields and agriculture-centric cities of the Missouri Valley. Because the regiment's soldiers knew what they were getting into and, more importantly, how long they would be asked to serve, the pace of recruiting was astounding. The training of the regiment was straightforward and effective. The regiment avoided training for maneuvers at higher levels in favor of building the capacity of the captains and lieutenants to lead smaller organizations in diverse operations. The focus on physical fitness, marksmanship, open order drill and discipline created an organization that was fully prepared to take on the physical rigor and complex tasks of a counterinsurgency fight.

In active combat, the 32nd Regiment proved the value of its training. Its soldiers endured the physical difficulty of the Philippine climate and terrain and overwhelmed the Philippine Army of Liberation in every recorded skirmish. Even if we ascribed some of the regiment's success to the disjointed leadership and poor marksmanship of the Filipinos, the 32nd's use of open-order tactics, aggressive action and from-the-front leadership action would likely have led to success even against a better prepared foe. As the 32nd settled into district life it transitioned from combat to civic tasks easily. The officers were comfortable with intent-based instructions and they used their personal knowledge of the population in their regions as they applied General Order Numbers 43 and 40. Based on Private White's diary, the soldiers were also comfortable with operations that included both combat and construction. They were fully capable of understanding that patrolling, building, teaching, and standing guard were all aspects of the same operation.

Topics for Further Research

While other authors have researched other regiments, there has yet to be published a depiction of the performance of the Federal Volunteer Regiments as a whole. Because of this gap, it cannot be assumed that the experiences of one regiment can speak to the entire system. In this light, it is possible that the 32nd was not extraordinary at all. It could have been a completely average organization, within a very successful assembly of regiments. The Philippine insurrection was a decentralized counterinsurgency operation, conducted in compartmented terrain, among a multi-tribal population. An overall characterization of the federal volunteers may not even be possible. Further study could focus on the similarities and differences between the federal volunteer regiments to determine if those traits this paper has ascribed to the 32nd were actually characteristics of the entire federal regimental volunteer system.

Future research could also be conducted to determine if the experiences of the federal volunteer regiments can inform current policymakers concerning the manning of military units, in a democratic society, for long-term counterinsurgency operations. In 1899, there was value in standing up entirely new regiments for a limited time period and for a specific counterinsurgency mission; does this concept have value today?

One thing is certain: for nineteen months, the 32nd Infantry Regiment (U.S.V.) operated successfully along the northern banks of Manila Bay in the United States Army's first successful counterinsurgency. Based on the history and experiences of the 32nd, the Army Act of 1899 created an effective organization that was capable of addressing both the political and the military problems of the Philippine Insurrection.

90

[1]William McKinley, *Annual Message of the President to Congress*, 3 December 1900, http://www.presidency.ucsb.edu/ws/index.php?pid=29541, The American Presidency Project, University of California, Santa Barbara, (accessed 21 Jan 2006).

BIBLIOGRAPHY

Books

Bell. William G., *Commanding Generals and Chiefs of Staff.* Washington D.C: Center of Military History, 1983.

Boot, Max. *The Savage Wars of Peace: Small Wars and the Rise of American Power.* New York: Basic Books, 2002.

Bain, David Haward. *Sitting in Darkness: Americans in the Philippines.* Boston: Houghton Mifflin Company, 1984.

Coffman, Edward M., *The Old Army: A Portrait of the American Army in Peacetime, 1784-1898.* New York: Oxford University Press, 1986.

Coffman, Edward M., *The Regulars: The American Army 1898-194.,* Cambridge, MA: Harvard University Press, 2004.

Cooper, Jerry, *The Rise of the National Guard.* Lincoln, Nebraska: University of Nebraska Press, 1997.

Cosmas, Graham A. *An Army For Empire: The United States Army in the Spanish American War.* Columbia, MO: University of Missouri Press, 1994.

Crane, Charles J., *The Experiences of a Colonel of Infantry.* New York: Knickerbocker Press, 1923.

Crouch, Thomas W., *A Leader of Volunteers: Frederick Funston and the 20th Kansas in the Philippines, 1898-1899.* Lawrence, KS: Coronado Press, 1984.

Feuer, A. B., *America at War: the Philippines, 1898-1913.* Westport, CT: Praeger, 2002.

Gates, John M., *Schoolbooks and Krags: The United States Army in the Philippines, 1898-1902.* Westport, CT: Greenwood Press, 1973.

Herman, Frederick J., *The Forty-second Foot: A History of the Forty-second Regiment of Infantry, United States Volunteers, organized for service in the Philippine insurrection. 1899-1900-1901*. Kansas City, MO: Forty Second Infantry Regiment U.S.V., 1945.

Langellier, J. P., *Uncle Sam's Little Wars: The Spanish-American War, Philippine Insurrection, and Boxer Rebellion, 1898-1902*. Mechanicsburg, Pa.: Stackpole Books, 1999.

Linn, Brian M., *The Philippine War, 1899-1902*. Lawrence, KS: University Press of Kansas, 2000.

Linn, Brian M., *The U.S. Army and Counterinsurgency in the Philippine War, 1899-1902*. Chapel Hill, NC: The University of North Carolina Press, 1989.

Mahan, Alfred T., *Lessons of the War with Spain and Other Articles*. Boston: Little, Brown, 1899.

Miller, Stuart C., *Benevolent Assimilation: The American Conquest of the Philippines, 1899-1903*. New Haven, CT: Yale University Press, 1982.

Morrison, Samuel E., *Dissent in Three American Wars.* Cambridge, MA: Harvard University Press, 1970.

Roddenbough, Theophilus F., ed., *The Army of the United States: Historical Sketches of Staff and Line with Portraits of Generals-in-Chief.* New York: Maynard, Merrill and Company, 1896.

Sexton William T., *Soldiers in the Philippines: a History of the Insurrection.* Washington: Infantry Journal, 1945.

Sexton, William T., *Soldiers in the Sun: An Adventure in Imperialism.* Harrisburg, PA: The Military Service Publishing Company, 1939.

Stewart, Richard W., ed., *American Military History Volume I: The United States Army and the Forging of a Nation, 1775-1917.* Center of Military History, Washington D.C., 2005.

United States Military Academy Association of Graduates, *Register of Graduates and Former Cadets of the United States Military Academy.* West Point, NY: Association of Graduates, USMA, 48th ed., 1993.

Upton, Emory. *The Military Policy of the United States from 1775.* Washington: Government Printing Office, 1904.

Walker, Dale L., *The Boys of '98: Theodore Roosevelt and the Rough Riders.* New York: Forge, 1998.

Warner, Ezra J., *Generals in Blue: Lives of the Union Commander.* Baton Rouge, LA: Louisiana State University Press, 1964.

Journal Articles

Montague Barlow, "The Economic Legislation of the Year 1899." *The Economic Journal*, Vol. 10, No. 37 (Mar., 1900), pp. 91-96.

Andrew J. Birtle, "The U.S. Army's Pacification of Marinduque, Philippine Islands, April 1900-April 1901." *The Journal of Military History*, Vol. 61, No. 2 (Apr., 1997), pp. 255-282.

Donald P. Boyer, Jr., "The Infantry of the Regular Army." *Military Affairs*, Vol. 11, No. 2 (Summer, 1947), pp. 103-115.

Graham A. Cosmas, "From Order to Chaos: The War Department, The National Guard, and Military Policy, 1898." *Military Affairs*, Vol. 29, No. 3 (Autumn, 1965), pp. 105-122.

Graham A. Cosmas, "Military Reform After the Spanish-American War: The Army Reorganization Fight of 1898-1899." *Military Affairs*, Vol. 35, No. 1 (Feb., 1971), pp. 12-18.

Timothy K. Deady, "Lessons from a Successful Counterinsurgency: The Philippines, 1899-1902." Parameters, Vol. 35, No 1. (Spring 2005), pp. 53-68.

Arthur A. Ekirch, Jr., "The Idea of a Citizen Army." *Military Affairs*, Vol. 17, No. 1 (Spring, 1953), pp. 30-36.

Brian M. Linn, "Provincial Pacification in the Philippines, 1900-1901: The First District Department of Northern Luzon." *Military Affairs*, Vol. 51, No. 2 (Apr., 1987), pp. 62-66.

Edward Ranson, "Nelson A. Miles as Commanding General, 1895-1903." *Military Affairs*, Vol. 29, No. 4. (Winter, 1965-1966), pp. 179-200.

William R. Shepherd, "Record of Political Events." *Political Science Quarterly*, Vol. 14, No. 4. (Dec., 1899), pp. 737-760.

Munroe Smith, "Record of Political Events." *Political Science Quarterly*, Vol. 14, No. 2. (Jun., 1899), pp. 357-388.

George J. Tanham, "Service Relations Sixty Years Ago." *Military Affairs*, Vol. 23, No. 3. (Autumn, 1959), pp. 139-148.

US Government Sources

Craig, Louis A. ed., *Roster of the Thirty-second Infantry: United States Volunteers: Colonel Louis A. Craig, Commanding, service, 1899, 1900, 1901*, Manila, *Philippine Islands*. Balanga, Baraan province, Island of Luzon: 32nd Regimental Headquarters, 1902

Compiled Military Service Records (CMSR), 32nd Infantry Regiment (U.S.V.). Record Group 94, National Archives and Records Administration, Washington, DC.

MacArthur, Arthur, *Annual Report of Major General Arthur MacArthur, U.S.V., Division of the Philippines*. Manila: 1901.

McKinley, William H., *Benevolent Assimilation Proclamation, December 21 1898*. The Philippine Centennial Celebration Website, Laguna, P.I., Available from http://www.msc.edu.ph/centennial/benevolent.html. Accessed 16 Jan 2006.

McKinley, William H., *Annual Message of the President to Congress, Dec 5 1898*. The American Presidency Project, University of California, Santa Barbara. Available from http://www.presidency.ucsb.edu/ws/print.php?pid=29539. Accessed 11 Jan 2006.

McKinley, William H., *Annual Message of the President to Congress, Dec 3 1900*. The American Presidency Project, University of California, Santa Barbara. Available from http://www.presidency.ucsb.edu/ws/print.php?pid=29541. Accessed 21 Jan 2006

United States. Adjutant-General's Office. *War of the Rebellion, Spanish-American War, Philippine Insurrection: summary of events of the War of the Rebellion, 1860-1865, Spanish-American War, Philippine Insurrection, 1898-1900, troubles in China, 1900, with other valuable information in regard to the various wars, compiled from official records*. Washington: Government Printing Office, 1905.

United States. Adjutant-General's Office. *Correspondence relating to the war with Spain: including the insurrection in the Philippine Islands and the China Relief Expedition, April 15, 1898, to July 30, 1902*. Washington: Government Printing Office, 1905.

Unites States Congress. Senate. *Report of the Commission Appointed by the President to Investigate the Conduct of the War Department in the War with Spain.* 56th Cong., 1st sess., 1900.

United States Congress. Senate, *Hearings on Affairs on the Philippine Islands.* Washington D.C.: 58th Congress, 1st sess., 1904.

United States. National Archives. *History of the Philippine Insurrection [microfilm] against the United States, 1899-1903: and documents relating to the War Department project for publishing the history.* Washington: unk.

United States. War Department, *Annual Reports of the War Department 1898.* Washington D.C.: Government Printing Office, 1899.

United States. War Department, *Annual Reports of the War Department 1899.* Washington D.C.: Government Printing Office, 1900.

United States War Department, *Infantry Drill Regulation, Extended Order Drill.* Washington D.C.: War Department, 1898.

Monographs, Theses And Unpublished Materials

Archives of the 32nd Volunteer Infantry Association, maintained at CARL, Special Collections, Ft Leavenworth KS.

Bustos, Marcellino, *Letter from Bustos to Judge of Elections, 15 September 1900,* Department of Northern Luzon, 5th District, NARA RG 395, E2092.

Craig, Louis A., *Consolidated Report of Schools for the Month of August 1900 in Territory Occupied by the 32nd Infantry U.S.V.* Reports of Schools: 5th District Department of Northern Luzon, NARA, RG395, E2303.

Craig, Louis A., *Consolidated Report of Schools for the Month of December 1900 in Territory Occupied by the 32nd Infantry U.S.V.* Reports of Schools: 5th District Department of Northern Luzon, NARA, RG395, E2303.

Craig, Louis A., *Report to the Secretary of War from the Thirty-Second Volunteer Infantry Regiment, COL Louis A. Craig, Commanding.* Personal collection of the Craig family, 1901.

Densmore, George A., *Letter from Densmore to Craig, 17 September 1900,* 5th District, Department of Northern Luzon, NARA RG 395, E2092.

Eckers, Frank W., *Letter from Eckers to Craig, 18 September 1900,* Department of Northern Luzon, 5th District, NARA RG 395, E2092.

Killingsworth, Charles, *Diary of Charles Killingsworth, Regimental Scouts, 32nd Infantry Regiment, United States Volunteers.* Fort Leavenworth, KS: Archives of the 32nd Infantry Regimental Association.

Linn, Brian M, *The Thirty-Third Infantry, United States Volunteers: an American regiment in the Philippine insurrection, 1899-1901.* Masters Thesis, The Ohio State University, 1981.

Peed, Henry, *Report that the only school in Orion is occupied by American Troops, 30 March 1901,* 5th District, Department of Northern Luzon, NARA RG 395 E. 2092 Box 2.

Strother, Lewis, *Telegram: Strother to Craig, 5 August 1900*, 5th District, Department of Northern Luzon, NARA RG 395, E2092.

White, Karl D. *The Philippine Insurrection: Diaries of Karl D. White, Company K, 32nd Volunteer Infantry, 1899-1901*. Fort Leavenworth, KS: Archives of the 32nd Infantry Regimental Association.